from *Freezer*

to

Instant Pot®

The Cookbook

Instant Pot®

from Freezer *to* Instant Pot®

The Cookbook

HOW TO COOK **No-Prep Meals**
IN YOUR INSTANT POT®

STRAIGHT FROM YOUR FREEZER

Bruce Weinstein and Mark Scarbrough

PHOTOGRAPHS BY ERIC MEDSKER

VORACIOUS
LITTLE, BROWN AND COMPANY
NEW YORK BOSTON LONDON

Little, Brown and Company
Hachette Book Group
1290 Avenue of the Americas, New York, NY 10104
littlebrown.com

First Edition: July 2019

Voracious is an imprint of Little, Brown and Company, a division of
Hachette Book Group, Inc. The Voracious name and logo are trademarks
of Hachette Book Group, Inc.

The publisher is not responsible for websites (or their content) that are
not owned by the publisher.

The Hachette Speakers Bureau provides a wide range of authors for
speaking events. To find out more, go to hachettespeakersbureau.com
or call (866) 376-6591.

Photographs © Eric Medsker
Interior design by Laura Palese

ISBN 978-0-316-42566-7
LCCN 2019935427

10 9 8 7 6 5 4 3 2 1

LSC-C

Printed in the United States of America

Contents

Introduction

THIS COOKBOOK IS THE HOLY GRAIL FOR BUSY PEOPLE,

for those of us who rush in the door
at the end of the day, pull a package of ice-crusted
whatever out of the freezer, and think,

"CAN I EAT THIS?"

Good news: If you've got an Instant Pot
and this book, the answer is "Yes!"

———————

This book is also for those of us who love to shop supermarket sales and to stock the freezer. (Those of us in the know raid the grocery store's meat case the day after any holiday.)

And it's for people who routinely shop at big-box stores and walk out with a twenty-pound bag of frozen chicken breasts and a five-pound bag of frozen bell pepper strips. We've got you covered.

In other words, this cookbook is the ultimate convenience tool for the Instant Pot. These recipes allow you to store meat, poultry, and seafood in your freezer until the very moment you want to start cooking — and then, *without thawing them at all,* make a meal in a fraction of the time you'd need to defrost, let alone cook, a conventional meal. Now *that's* the power of your Instant Pot pressure cooker.

Plus, we give you options galore! In most of these recipes, you can choose to use frozen *or* fresh vegetables (more on that in a bit — but never *thawed* frozen vegetables). Whenever possible, we expand the range of the recipes by giving you the choice to use fresh *or* dried herbs; and sometimes you've got the option to select from among several flavorful cooking liquids for the dish. Then there are the "road map" recipes that let you customize a classic dish exactly to your taste (and your pantry).

Let us repeat: *You need not prep food in advance for any recipe in this book.* You can use frozen vegetables and a frozen cut of meat *as is*. And you'll *never* need to cut items up, mix them in a storage bag, freeze the thing, and cook it later on.

Sure, you can do a little prep if you want. If you've bought fresh meat on sale and want to freeze it, it will save you time later to remove the packaging as well as any "diaper" next to the meat (for more on that, see page 5). If necessary, cut the meat to the right size for use in a chosen recipe, then seal it in a storage bag and put it in the freezer for a couple of months until you're ready to prepare the meal.

Or go a little further and put all the *frozen* fare for a recipe in a storage bag, then seal it and store it in the freezer until you're ready to make dinner. However, please take note: Because we calibrated these recipes to work with room-temperature or refrigerated broths and other cooking liquids, you cannot put *all* the ingredients for a recipe in a pre-prepped bag. But why would you want to go to all that trouble anyway? This book is about making things *easy*.

So much good news, right? But let's be honest about this special way to cook a meal in the Instant Pot. Yes, there's a lot of social media chatter about cooking frozen fare in America's favorite appliance. Well-meaning people offer advice like "just throw it in and add a couple of minutes."

Maybe. We tried that. A lot. And we ended up with some horrifying results. Luckily for you, we ran so many kitchen experiments that we were able to create a chart with basic guidelines for cooking *anything* from frozen in your pot (see pages 12–19).

All of which brings up a basic question: Why's it so hard to develop a perfect recipe for cooking a meal straight from frozen?

First, frozen foods throw off a great deal of moisture as they thaw in the pot, swamping casseroles and braises. Sure, you can toss a bag of frozen chicken breasts in a casserole. But because of all the released liquid, you'll probably end up with rice *soup,* no matter what you wanted.

Second, frozen foods cook at different times in the pot based on the thickness and *density* (not the weight) of the meat or vegetable. The advice to "add a few minutes" is decent enough for frozen boneless skinless chicken breasts (although we do have a way to make these better on pages 74–75). But that advice is mere drivel when it comes to a frozen round roast or a pork loin that ends up tough at its edges but cold (and raw) at its center.

And third, frozen *ground* meat presents a host of problems, including the fact that the meat stays in a lump even after it has cooked. Truth be told, working with a block of ground beef is not as simple as it sounds. We'll explain more in our techniques section below — and much more in the headnotes to specific recipes.

In fact, many of the challenges facing frozen-to-dinner dishes are recipe-specific. There's no one set of rules to cover the many (and sometimes strange) variables at play. (Frozen ground turkey ends up in strings!) In our general timing chart for common foods, our guidelines are for the specific cut on its own, not that cut in a dish with other ingredients.

In other words, most of the culinary education in this book happens in the recipes themselves — and specifically in the recipe headnotes. Yes, some of those prattle on a bit. But don't skip them. You'll learn *why* you need to treat your ingredients a certain way for each dish. After you've cooked a few recipes, you'll be able to customize them as you like, using ours as templates.

But before you get cooking, we'll offer some notes on general techniques, then we'll answer a few Frequently Asked Questions (that is, FAQs).

But take note: The basic operation of the pot as well as the ins and outs of pressure cooking itself are missing from this introduction and the chapter introductions. Read the pot's manual. And consider joining one of the Instant Pot Facebook groups where you can get all your questions answered. (We're active in two of the biggest.) And check out our previous book, *The Instant Pot Bible,* for a much fuller introduction that delves into the scientific explanations and culinary tricks for making great food from one of the world's favorite appliances.

Read These Nine Important Technique Notes Before You Get Started

1. Use our weights and volumes.

If you don't, whatever you've got frozen may not fit in the pot. Thawed meat and vegetables are bendable; frozen stuff is rigid. In other words, a larger cut of meat than we call for might not fit in the pot. Besides, using the recipe's stated weights and volumes is more important in pressure cooking than in oven cooking and *way* more important when cooking stuff from frozen because things must thaw *and* cook. One warning in advance: Pay particular attention to the size of bone-in or boneless skinless chicken breasts in the recipes.

2. Watch that MAX FILL line.

Frozen proteins are like icebergs. They sit in the sauce or braising ingredients and give off lots of water and other liquid as they warm up (that is, melt). If all the ingredients start out near the MAX FILL line inside the pot's insert, they may be well above it when the frozen fare thaws — and thus may cause the pot to fail. Don't add ingredients willy-nilly or double the amounts unless you're sure there will be room for everything when the frozen stuff thaws.

3. Always remove the packaging from frozen food before cooking it.

We haven't included this step in any recipe — and yes, it's a pain in the neck. Slicing off the plastic wrapper and removing the Styrofoam container are generally not a big problem. But then there's what's called in butcher parlance the "diaper," the little pad under the meat that's made to absorb juices and liquid the cut may give off as it sits in the supermarket's case. That diaper is tearable, even friable. Worse yet, it's full of a gel that's downright gross. Most of the time it peels neatly off beef and pork; unfortunately, it sticks like mad to poultry of all sorts.

Our best advice is to run the frozen block of chicken thighs or ground turkey under lukewarm water as you peel off the diaper in bits and pieces. Once you tear the diaper, it will leak a foam into your sink. You'll want to clean your sink well afterwards. You'll also need to nick some of the gel off the frozen meat with a paring knife (still under running water). Leave none of that gunk behind. You don't want it in your dinner.

4. Be prepared to take extra steps to control soupiness, our bane when we were creating recipes for this book.

There's no way to predict how much frozen water or other liquids are stored in any given package of frozen ground beef or bone-in chicken breasts. For example, chicken "injected with a solution" will release all of that solution into the pot as the meat thaws. And kosher chicken, which is essentially prebrined, stores lots more salty water in its meat than standard North American chicken does.

If a dish ends up soupier than you like, turn on the SAUTÉ function to MEDIUM, NORMAL, or CUSTOM 300°F after cooking under pressure and boil the stew or braise down a bit, stirring quite often. Sorry about this — we were able to eliminate most of the variables here, but this one proved intractable. We provide the timing that most often worked in testing.

Remember, too, that rice and pasta continue to absorb liquid after cooking — which means dishes that contain them may need to be set aside for only 5 minutes with the lid askew before the meal "tightens" up to the right consistency.

5. Break up frozen ground beef after it's cooked.

As we indicated, frozen ground meat stays in a block, even after cooking under pressure. Breaking that block up is a bit of a chore. We suggest holding the block of cooked meat with a meat fork, then using the edge of a metal cooking spoon to break the block into smaller and smaller bits right in the pot's insert — often down to the size of mini meatballs but sometimes even smaller (the individual recipes will guide you).

You can also lift the block of cooked meat out of the pot with kitchen tongs, put it on a nearby cutting board (preferably one with a trough at its edge), and use a knife to cut the ground meat into smaller bits, even shreds. In many cases, the meat will still be pink or red inside. No worries! In these recipes, the shredded meat undergoes a second cooking (either with the SAUTÉ function or under pressure), so the ground beef or turkey will eventually be cooked through.

6. Invest in a pair of kitchen shears.

They are the easiest way to cut up chicken thighs or tenders right in the pot. They're also terrific at cutting ground beef into small bits in the pot. We call for them in any recipe only as an alternative technique, but we put the advice here in the hope you'll spend ten bucks for a tool that can make these recipes even easier.

7. Use a rack or vegetable steamer *only* when necessary.

In most (but not all) cases, we use a rack or a large, open vegetable steamer to *protect* delicate or starchy ingredients sitting in the liquid underneath. (For another way to get around this problem, which can lead to the pot flashing its burn indicator, see note 8 below.)

Here's the problem: Frozen foods take longer to come to pressure when they sit directly in a liquid. The food is super cold, the broth (or whatever) is at room temperature, and the frozen fare chills it — which means it takes longer to come to a boil, produce steam, and get the pot to pressure. However, once all that happens, the actual time under pressure is often *shorter* than recipes that use fresh or thawed meat because the frozen stuff has been sitting longer in liquid that has been steadily warming up. In other words, the frozen stuff has been cooking long before the pot comes to pressure.

By contrast, when frozen fare sits on a rack or a steamer in the pot, the liquid takes about the normal time to boil and produce steam under the meat — so the actual cooking time under pressure is now longer (because the meat wasn't sitting in liquid getting increasingly warm as the cut thawed). Pay attention to the specifics of each recipe.

When we say the "pot's rack" in a recipe, we mean the trivet that came with your machine. If you've lost yours or you have an older model without a trivet, order one. Or use a vegetable steamer that fits in the pot. In fact, for a couple of the rice casseroles in this book, you *must* use a large, open vegetable steamer (and not the rack or trivet) because these dishes use more liquid than some others and a steamer has taller feet that allow the frozen fare to sit up higher out of the liquid.

8. **Sometimes, you must heat liquid until wisps of steam rise off it before adding the frozen food and putting the food under pressure.**

This step is important when you're dealing with starchy foods like rice and pasta. A block of frozen chicken thighs drops the temperature of the liquid in the pot so much that it takes longer to come to a boil and then gives any grains of rice or bits of pasta a chance to stick to the pot's bottom before they start to dance in the boil. Therefore, you *must* heat the liquid to give it a head start on getting to a boil (and thus getting the pot to pressure) once you lock on the lid. In some cases, we take care of the "temperature drop" problem with a rack or a vegetable steamer (as in note 7). But in others, we set the frozen meat right in the liquid because we want to give it a braised (rather than a steamed) texture.

Why do we say to heat until you see "*many* or *several* wisps of steam?" Why don't we just suggest bringing the liquid to a simmer? Because we don't want to lose too much to evaporation. Wisps of steam are enough to ensure the success of the dish.

9. **Note the difference in cooking times between items out of a standard freezer, which is usually set at 0°F, and those from a chest or "deep freeze" freezer, which is usually set at –20°F.** In most recipes, this difference in freezers makes no difference in cooking. (We tested every recipe with cuts at both temperatures to make sure.) But in some recipes, particularly those that use large or dense cuts of meat, the difference can be pronounced. Every recipe will tell you if you need to adjust the timing for foods that come out of a colder chest freezer. But please note: If your *chest* freezer is set at only 0°F, you don't need to adjust the recipe.

A Few FAQs

1. **Must I use frozen vegetables?** No. Most of the recipes were written so that you *can* use frozen (but not thawed) vegetables. Throughout the book, we'll indicate when you can use frozen or fresh, whichever you have on hand. In a few instances, we'll tell you when *only* frozen vegetables will work (because of timing in all cases). And we never call for frozen root

vegetables *except* butternut squash cubes or unseasoned hash brown cubes (in which case the fresh vegetables will *not* work with the timing given).

By the way, if you buy prepped fresh vegetables from the supermarket (like chopped onion or celery), use the volume amounts stated for the frozen vegetables.

2. Where's the frozen ground pork in these recipes?

We found that casseroles and stews were just too greasy when we used ground pork. (We make an exception for the burger road map on pages 110–11 and suggest that you can use a 50-50 combo of ground beef and ground pork.) But tastes indeed vary. You might find ground pork more to your liking in any recipe. Or ground veal. Or ground goat. In all cases, there's no change in the timing if the weight of the block of frozen ground meat is the same.

3. You always call for white basmati rice. Will other long-grain white rices work?

Yes, so long as they are not "converted" or "instant" rice. But many other varietals, particularly the generic long-grain white rice sold under a supermarket's in-house brand, turn mushy under pressure. White basmati stands up more consistently. We allowed ourselves a bit of fussiness with this one ingredient. By the way, you *cannot* substitute medium-grain white rice like Arborio or brown rice of any sort for the white basmati rice without major alterations to the recipe. Mostly, these other rices will not work with the liquid and timings given.

4. Why are the timing charts in the recipes divided into two lines?

The lines differentiate between cooking a dish in the newer Max Instant Pot (which cooks at 15 psi, roughly the same pressure as a stovetop pressure cooker) and all the former models (which cook at 12.1 psi for HIGH). If you have a Max, you can use the top row of the chart. Everyone else needs to use the second row, pressing the appropriate button (or simply HIGH PRESSURE) as indicated by the recipe.

By the way, the Max machine *does* allow you to set the pot for the older HIGH setting — and you can certainly do so with these recipes, using the second line of the chart for your Max machine, thereby cooking at a slightly lower pressure (and a longer time) in your newer-model machine.

5. Why do some recipes give the instructions for only a 6-quart cooker?

Look in the *Beyond* section to find the adaptation necessary for an 8-quart pot. In almost all cases, you *must* make this adaptation. (We'll let you know when you can but don't have to.)

6. Where's the option for a 3-quart cooker, the way you had it in your other Instant Pot book?

We nixed it because we felt this method of cooking was impractical in the smaller cooker. First, a frozen lump of chicken thighs or a rock-solid chuck roast won't fit. Second, it's hard to find ½-pound packages of frozen ground meat (so the recipe for the smaller cooker would *require* you to plan in advance, dividing and freezing that 1-pound package of ground beef). And third, the amount of released liquid from the thawed meat plus the broth or other liquids required to bring the smaller pot to pressure often ended up swamping the dish.

7. What about a 5-quart Instant Pot?

For a limited time, Instant Pot made a 5-quart model. That model is long out of production, so we've crafted this book for the Instant Pots currently on the market. Every recipe (except one — the frozen turkey breast) can be made in a 6- or an 8-quart model.

If you have a 5-quart pot, you may be able to prepare some of the recipes using the stated ingredients for a 6-quart pot, particularly the soups and stews. But be careful not to fill the pot over its MAX FILL line. Most of the pasta and rice recipes will cause sputtering during a quick release in the 5-quart pot. Some may even cause excessive foaming and make the pot fail.

8. You had a slow-cooking option for hundreds of recipes in *The Instant Pot Bible*. Why not here?

Because despite a million internet videos to the contrary, the USDA *does not recommend* cooking frozen fare in a slow cooker. Basically, the food sits too long at an unsafe temperature. Yes, by the time the slow cooker heats up and cooks for several hours, it may kill the pests (or most of them, depending on what has grown in that oversized petri dish). But even putting an end to the bad stuff doesn't solve your problems. The bugs', um, "residue" can make you ill. Please be safe. No dinner's worth a hospital stay.

That said, the Pot Pie road map does use the SLOW COOK function to cook the biscuit topping once it's put over the stew.

Let's Get Cooking!

There's a lot of great food to be had right out of the freezer when you've got an Instant Pot on the counter. Just remember the basic safety tips outlined in the machine's manual (keep electric cords away from water, don't jostle the pot while it cooks, etc.). And be prepared to make choices in these recipes.

We'd love to hear about your adventures. Look us up on Facebook (Bruce Weinstein in Colebrook, Connecticut, and Mark Scarbrough, writer), on Twitter (@bruceweinstein and @markscarbrough), and/or on Instagram (@bruceaweinstein and @markscarbrough). Or drop us a note on our website, bruceandmark.com. Or check out our YouTube channel, Cooking with Bruce and Mark, for lots of step-by-step videos for the recipes in this book and our previous one. We're happy to help. And, mostly, to connect.

A Master Guide

TO COOKING

STRAIGHT FROM THE FREEZER
IN THE INSTANT POT

FROZEN ITEM	Use a rack or metal vegetable steamer in the pot?	Add how much water or broth?	MAX pressure cooking time from a 0°F freezer	
Beef, burger patties, 6 oz. each (up to 4)	Yes	1½ cups	22 minutes for pink or 25 minutes for no pink	
Beef, chuck roast, 2 lbs.	No	2 cups	1 hour 20 minutes	
Beef, chuck roast, 3 lbs.	No	2 cups	1 hour 30 minutes	
Beef, corned brisket, 3 lbs.	Yes	1½ cups	1 hour 20 minutes	
Beef, eye of round, 2 lbs.	No	2 cups	55 minutes for pink or 1 hour 5 minutes for no pink	
Beef, eye of round, 3 lbs.	No	2 cups	1 hour 5 minutes for pink or 1 hour 12 minutes for no pink	
Beef, flank steak (folded in half or thirds), 2 lbs.	No	2 cups	1 hour 10 minutes	
Beef, ground, 1 lb.	Yes	1½ cups	24 minutes for pink or 30 minutes for no pink	
Beef, ground, one 2-lb. block	Yes	1½ cups	34 minutes for pink or 37 minutes for no pink	

Say you just want to cook something out of the freezer right now, without consulting a specific recipe. This chart is your guide. The timings that follow are based on cooking a cut of meat or a lump of seafood either *in* liquid or *on a rack (or in a large, open vegetable steamer)* over liquid. They are for the meat or seafood *alone,* not with other ingredients.

You'll note that some of the timings here are different from those in individual recipes in this book. Sauce ingredients, vegetables, the viscosity of some liquids, and the coatings on a cut affect the timings in a recipe loaded with other ingredients.

These timings and amounts work in either a **6- or 8-quart Instant Pot.**

MAX pressure cooking time from a −20°F chest freezer	HIGH pressure cooking time from a 0°F freezer	HIGH pressure cooking time from a −20°F chest freezer	Release method
25 minutes for pink or 28 minutes for no pink	25 minutes for pink or 28 minutes for no pink	27 minutes for pink or 30 minutes for no pink	Quick
1 hour 30 minutes	1 hour 30 minutes	1 hour 40 minutes	Natural
1 hour 40 minutes	1 hour 40 minutes	1 hour 50 minutes	Natural
1 hour 30 minutes	1 hour 30 minutes	1 hour 40 minutes	Natural
1 hour for pink or 1 hour 10 minutes for no pink	1 hour for pink or 1 hour 20 minutes for no pink	1 hour 10 minutes for pink or 1 hour 20 minutes for no pink	Natural
1 hour 10 minutes for pink or 1 hour 15 minutes for no pink	1 hour 10 minutes for pink or 1 hour 15 minutes for no pink	1 hour 20 minutes for pink or 1 hour 30 minutes for no pink	Natural
1 hour 10 minutes	1 hour 20 minutes	1 hour 20 minutes	Natural
27 minutes for pink or 33 minutes for no pink	27 minutes for pink or 33 minutes for no pink	30 minutes for pink or 36 minutes for no pink	Quick
37 minutes for pink or 43 minutes for no pink	37 minutes for pink or 43 minutes for no pink	40 minutes for pink or 45 minutes for no pink	Quick

FROZEN ITEM	Use a rack or metal vegetable steamer in the pot?	Add how much water or broth?	MAX pressure cooking time from a 0°F freezer	
Beef, shaved, 1 lb.	No	2 cups	7 minutes	
Beef, shaved, one 2-lb. block	No	2 cups	12 minutes	
Beef, short ribs, bone-in, 8 oz. each (up to 6)	No	2 cups	37 minutes	
Beef, stew meat, 1 lb.	No	2 cups	40 minutes	
Beef, stew meat, 2 lbs.	No	2 cups	44 minutes	
Beef, top or bottom round roast, 2½ lbs.	Yes	1½ cups	1 hour	
Beef, top or bottom round roast, 3½ lbs.	Yes	1½ cups	1 hour 10 minutes	
Chicken breasts, bone-in, 10–12 oz. each (up to 4)	No	2 cups	35 minutes	
Chicken breasts, boneless skinless, 5–6 oz. each (up to 6)	Yes	1½ cups	12 minutes	
Chicken breasts, boneless skinless, 10–12 oz. each (up to 6)	Yes	1½ cups	20 minutes	
Chicken tenders, 1- to 2-lb. block	Yes	1½ cups	12 minutes	
Chicken thighs, boneless skinless, 2 lbs.	No	2 cups	18 minutes	
Chicken wings, 1–3 lbs.	No	2 cups	12 minutes	
Chicken, whole, 4 lbs.	Yes	1½ cups	55 minutes	
Fish fillets (white-fleshed), thick, such as halibut, mahi-mahi, or cod, 6 oz. each (up to 4)	Yes	1½ cups	8 minutes	
Game hens, whole, 1–1¼ lbs. each (up to 2)	No	2 cups	30 minutes	
Meatballs, dinner size and precooked (turkey, pork, or beef), 1–1½ oz. each, up to 1½ lbs. total weight	No	2 cups	5 minutes	

MAX pressure cooking time from a −20°F chest freezer	HIGH pressure cooking time from a 0°F freezer	HIGH pressure cooking time from a −20°F chest freezer	Release method
9 minutes	9 minutes	11 minutes	Quick
14 minutes	14 minutes	16 minutes	Quick
40 minutes	40 minutes	45 minutes	Natural
45 minutes	45 minutes	48 minutes	Natural
47 minutes	47 minutes	50 minutes	Natural
1 hour 7 minutes	1 hour 7 minutes	1 hour 20 minutes	Natural
1 hour 17 minutes	1 hour 17 minutes	1 hour 30 minutes	Natural
40 minutes	40 minutes	45 minutes	Quick
12 minutes	15 minutes	15 minutes	Quick
23 minutes	23 minutes	25 minutes	Quick
12 minutes	15 minutes	15 minutes	Quick
20 minutes	20 minutes	22 minutes	Natural
12 minutes	15 minutes	15 minutes	Quick
1 hour 5 minutes	1 hour 5 minutes	1 hour 15 minutes	Natural
10 minutes	10 minutes	12 minutes	Quick
35 minutes	40 minutes	45 minutes	Natural
5 minutes	7 minutes	7 minutes	Quick

FROZEN ITEM	Use a rack or metal vegetable steamer in the pot?	Add how much water or broth?	MAX pressure cooking time from a 0°F freezer
Meatballs, mini and precooked (turkey, pork, or beef), ½–1 oz. each, up to 2 lbs. total weight	No	2 cups	3 minutes
Pork, bone-in chops, 8 oz. each (up to 4)	Yes	2 cups	22 minutes
Pork, center-cut boneless chops, 6 oz. each (up to 4)	Yes	2 cups	20 minutes
Pork, loin roast, 2 lbs. (fat side up)	No	2 cups	32 minutes
Pork, loin roast, 3 lbs. (fat side up)	No	2 cups	37 minutes
Pork, shoulder, bone-in, 3½ lbs.	No	2 cups	2 hours
Pork, shoulder, boneless, 3½ lbs.	No	2 cups	1 hour 55 minutes
Pork, smoked ham, boneless, precooked, 3½ lbs.	Yes	1½ cups	35 minutes
Pork, smoked ham steaks, precooked, 8 oz. each (up to 3)	Yes	2 cups	3 minutes
Pork, stew meat, 2 lbs.	No	2 cups	37 minutes
Pork, stew meat, 3 lbs.	No	2 cups	40 minutes
Salmon fillets, skin on or skinless, 6 oz. each (up to 4)	Yes	1½ cups	5 minutes
Sausage, bulk (beef, pork, or turkey), 1 lb.	Yes	1½ cups	30 minutes
Sausage, bulk (beef, pork, or turkey), one 2-lb. block	Yes	1½ cups	37 minutes
Sausage links (beef, pork, or turkey), smoked and precooked, 1–2 lbs.	Yes	1½ cups	10 minutes
Sausage links (beef, pork, or turkey), raw, 1–2 lbs.	No	1 cup	8 minutes

MAX pressure cooking time from a −20°F chest freezer	HIGH pressure cooking time from a 0°F freezer	HIGH pressure cooking time from a −20°F chest freezer	Release method
3 minutes	5 minutes	5 minutes	Quick
22 minutes	27 minutes	27 minutes	Quick
20 minutes	25 minutes	25 minutes	Quick
40 minutes	40 minutes	48 minutes	Natural
47 minutes	47 minutes	55 minutes	Natural
2 hours 15 minutes	2 hours 10 minutes	2 hours 25 minutes	Natural
2 hours 5 minutes	2 hours 5 minutes	2 hours 18 minutes	Natural
45 minutes	45 minutes	55 minutes	Natural
3 minutes	4 minutes	4 minutes	Quick
42 minutes	42 minutes	45 minutes	Natural
45 minutes	45 minutes	48 minutes	Natural
6 minutes	6 minutes	7 minutes	Quick
33 minutes	33 minutes	36 minutes	Quick
43 minutes	43 minutes	46 minutes	Quick
12 minutes	12 minutes	14 minutes	Quick
10 minutes	10 minutes	12 minutes	Quick

FROZEN ITEM	Use a rack or metal vegetable steamer in the pot?	Add how much water or broth?	MAX pressure cooking time from a 0°F freezer
Sea scallops, 1–2 lbs.	No	2 cups	0 minutes (see page 163)
Shrimp, raw, medium (about 30 per pound), 1–2 lbs.	No	2 cups	0 minutes (see page 163)
Smoked, fully cooked, bone-in meat, such as a turkey leg or ham hock, 10–12 oz. each (up to 2)	No	2 cups	40 minutes
Turkey, breast cutlets, 4 oz. each (up to 6)	Yes	2 cups	12 minutes
Turkey, breast, whole (skin on or off), 6 lbs.	No	2 cups	1 hour 12 minutes
Turkey, burger patties, 6 oz. each (up to 4)	Yes	1½ cups	25 minutes for no pink
Turkey, ground, 1 lb.	Yes	1½ cups	30 minutes
Turkey, ground, one 2-lb. block	Yes	1½ cups	37 minutes

One final note: Always take the internal temperature of a cut of meat after cooking with this method. Insert an instant-read meat thermometer into the center of the thickest section of the cut without touching any bone. If the temperature registers below the guidelines on the opposite page, put the lid back on the pot and cook for another 3 to 5 minutes under pressure, followed by the release method we've recommended.

MAX pressure cooking time from a −20°F chest freezer	HIGH pressure cooking time from a 0°F freezer	HIGH pressure cooking time from a −20°F chest freezer	Release method
0 minutes (see page 163)	0 minutes (see page 163)	0 minutes (see page 163)	Quick
0 minutes (see page 163)	0 minutes (see page 163)	0 minutes (see page 163)	Quick
40 minutes	50 minutes	50 minutes	Natural
12 minutes	15 minutes	15 minutes	Quick
1 hour 20 minutes	1 hour 20 minutes	1 hour 30 minutes	Natural
28 minutes for no pink	28 minutes for no pink	30 minutes for no pink	Quick
33 minutes	33 minutes	36 minutes	Quick
43 minutes	43 minutes	46 minutes	Quick

CURRENT USDA GUIDELINES FOR INTERNAL TEMPERATURES

Beef, Pork, Veal, or Lamb	Whole Muscle Meat	145°F and rest for 3 minutes
Beef, Pork, Veal, or Lamb	Ground	160°F
All Poultry	Whole Muscle or Ground	165°F

1

Soup

This book starts with dishes that many people consider the epitome of comfort food. But there are even more reasons to love soup made from the freezer in an Instant Pot. For one thing, a soup is less prone to failure and more forgiving because there's so much liquid in the mix. It's a rich bath for proteins, vegetables, and herbs.

For another, a soup is forgiving when it comes to the amounts of herbs, spices, and other flavorings in the mix. You can do a lot of "swapping out" in these recipes. And you can up the herbs and/or garlic as you like (or decrease them).

Plus, barring concerns about mushy pasta, you can hardly overcook a soup. What's another minute or two under pressure? What's an hour left on the KEEP WARM setting? Not much, to be honest.

However, you can *undercook* a soup. The protein can still be tough or raw. If you find that the meat isn't tender, give a soup a few more minutes under pressure, whether at MAX or HIGH, followed by the sort of release indicated in the original recipe. Again, that extra time won't do damage to the soup. If anything, it'll deepen the flavors.

Since you can't trim the fat from, say, frozen beef cubes, some of these soups end up a little richer than you might like. Defatting a soup before serving it is a matter of preference. There are fat separators sold for broths and such. To use one, you'll need to remove everything from the pot with a slotted spoon, then pour the soup base into the separator. Frankly, we think doing so is too much work for a pot of soup made with a frozen block of meat. When we want to defat a soup, we just skim its surface with a large cooking spoon. Besides, a little fat brings out more of the flavors in a soup. Now that's comfort food!

Road Map: **Bean Soup**

6–8 servings

1½ quarts (6 cups) broth of any type

Choose from chicken, beef, turkey, or vegetable broth — or a combination of any of these.

½ cup frozen chopped onion; or 1 small yellow or white onion, peeled and chopped

1½ tablespoons dried seasoning blend

Choose from Italian, French, Provençal, Cajun, Creole, poultry, or other purchased dried herb and spice blends.

2 pounds frozen smoked, bone-in meat

Choose from a large smoked turkey leg, smoked turkey wings, smoked pork hock, or a leftover smoked ham bone with plenty of meat on it.

1 pound (4 to 5 cups) frozen unseasoned chopped mixed vegetables

Choose one or more from broccoli florets, cauliflower florets, artichoke heart quarters, corn, lima beans, bell pepper strips, or any blend of frozen mixed vegetables you like; but avoid frozen, chopped leafy greens.

Two 15-ounce cans beans of any variety, drained and rinsed (3½ cups)

Choose *one or several* from red kidney, white, great northern, cannellini, navy, or just about any other bean you like, even chickpeas.

Here's the first road map recipe in this book. If you have *The Instant Pot Bible,* you know how to handle these variations. If you don't own that book (*what?!*), here's how to proceed: Take your pick from our preferred choices listed after each ingredient (or venture out on your own if you stay within the parameters given). Cook with a pen or pencil nearby so you can make notes on this page to remember next time what you did this time (for future success or improvements).

We didn't use dried beans with the frozen meat because we found they fell to the bottom of the pot and too often burned as the frozen meat thawed and the liquid came to a boil. The failures weren't worth the risk. So this recipe is a two-step process: First, make a rich stock with the frozen meat; then add canned beans to turn that stock into a soup.

Always rinse those canned beans in a strainer or sieve set in the sink. Canned beans can have a slimy coating of sugars that then dissolve in the soup and give it a slippery texture.

And one other note: There's no added salt in the recipe. Smoked meats are often loaded with it. You can pass more salt at the table.

1. Stir the broth, onion, and seasoning blend in a **6- or 8-quart Instant Pot.** Add the frozen meat, then lock the lid onto the pot.

2.

Set the machine for	Set the level for	The valve must be	Set the time for	If necessary, press
PRESSURE COOK	MAX	—	40 minutes with the KEEP WARM setting off	START
BEAN/CHILI, SOUP/BROTH, PRESSURE COOK, or MANUAL	HIGH	Closed	50 minutes with the KEEP WARM setting off	START

3. When the machine has finished cooking, turn it off and let the pressure **return to normal naturally,** 35–45 minutes, maybe even a little longer for dense meats like a smoked hock. Unlatch the lid and open the cooker.

4. Use tongs or a slotted spoon and a meat fork to transfer the meat to a nearby cutting board. Cool a few minutes, then shred the meat off the bone. Chop the meat into spoon-sized bits. Stir these back into the soup along with the frozen vegetables and canned beans. (Discard the bone and any fatty blobs you don't want in the soup.) Lock the lid back onto the pot.

5.

Set the machine for	Set the level for	The valve must be	Set the time for	If necessary, press
PRESSURE COOK	MAX	—	3 minutes with the KEEP WARM setting off	START
BEAN/CHILI, SOUP/BROTH, PRESSURE COOK, or MANUAL	HIGH	Closed	5 minutes with the KEEP WARM setting off	START

6. Use the **quick-release method** to bring the pot's pressure back to normal. Unlatch the lid and open the pot. Stir well before serving.

 Using a **-20°F CHEST FREEZER?** There is no difference in cooking times.

Beyond

- If desired (but you don't have to), you can increase all the ingredients by 50 percent for an **8-quart pot.**

- Omit the purchased seasoning blend and substitute 1½ teaspoons mild paprika, 1 teaspoon dried sage, 1 teaspoon dried thyme, ½ teaspoon celery seeds, and ½ teaspoon dried oregano.

- For more heat, add up to 2 teaspoons red pepper flakes with the seasoning blend (but make sure the blend you use has no cayenne in the mix).

- To add cheese to the soup, either add the rind from a wedge of Parmigiano-Reggiano with the vegetables and beans in step 4, or sprinkle the top of the hot soup with grated Monterey Jack or Swiss cheese after stirring the soup in step 6. In this second case, set the lid back on the pot without engaging the pressure valve for 5 minutes to melt the cheese.

- Garnish with dollops of sour cream and/or spoonfuls of pickle relish.

Chicken Noodle Soup

4–6 servings

1½ quarts (6 cups) chicken broth

1 cup <u>frozen</u> chopped onions; or
1 medium yellow or white
onion, peeled and chopped

2 teaspoons peeled and minced
garlic, optional

2 teaspoons stemmed fresh
thyme leaves, or 1 teaspoon
dried thyme

2 teaspoons stemmed and
minced fresh dill fronds, or
1 teaspoon dried dill

½ teaspoon table salt

1½ pounds <u>frozen</u> chicken
tenders

10 ounces <u>frozen</u> sliced carrots
(2 cups); or 3 medium fresh
carrots, thinly sliced

6 ounces regular, no-yolk, or
gluten-free dried egg noodles

The world's best chicken soup is made with dark-meat chicken on the bone. But it sure isn't the quickest. For this convenient and still-delicious classic chicken noodle, we've opted for chicken tenders because they cook quickly. No, they don't dry out in this technique because they're thawing *as* they begin to cook — and are then done in a flash.

If you've bought a large bag (say, 4 pounds) of fresh chicken tenders, you must first freeze 1½ pounds of it in a clump (in a sealed plastic bag, of course) to make this soup. It's very hard to break a giant block of frozen chicken tenders into a chunk that's the right weight. Trust us: We cracked the edge of a sink breaking a block apart.

1. Stir the broth, onion, garlic (if using), thyme, dill, and salt in a **6- or 8-quart Instant Pot.** Set the block of frozen tenders in the pot (it may partially rest against the side of the insert). Lock the lid onto the pot.

2.

Set the machine for	Set the level for	The valve must be	And set the time for	If necessary, press
PRESSURE COOK	MAX	—	6 minutes with the KEEP WARM setting off	START
SOUP/BROTH, POULTRY, PRESSURE COOK, or MANUAL	HIGH	Closed	8 minutes with the KEEP WARM setting off	START

3. Use the **quick-release method** to bring the pot's pressure back to normal. Unlatch the lid and open the cooker.

4. Break up the chicken in the pot. For the neatest pieces, use poultry or kitchen shears to cut the tenders into spoon-sized pieces. Or use the edge of a metal cooking spoon to break up the tenders (although this method requires wrist strength and a little sweaty determination.) Stir in the carrots and noodles. Lock the lid back onto the pot.

5.

Set the machine for	Set the level for	The valve must be	And set the time for	If necessary, press
PRESSURE COOK	MAX	—	3 minutes with the KEEP WARM setting off	START
SOUP/BROTH, PRESSURE COOK, or MANUAL	HIGH	Closed	4 minutes with the KEEP WARM setting off	START

6. Use the **quick-release method** to bring the pot's pressure back to normal. Unlatch the lid and open the cooker. Stir the soup well before serving.

 Using a **-20°F CHEST FREEZER?** There is no difference in cooking times.

Beyond

- For a heartier soup, add up to 2 cups frozen mixed vegetables with the frozen carrots.

- For a more complex flavor, use 5 cups chicken broth and 1 cup dry white wine.

- Ginger is a nice touch (especially if you've got the sniffles): Add up to 1 tablespoon peeled and minced fresh ginger with the onion.

- Ever tried a ham bone in chicken noodle soup? It adds a distinct meatiness. Add a *thawed* ham bone with a little bit of meat (not gobs) on it when you add the chicken. And omit the salt, since most hams are salty.

Butternut Squash Bisque

4–6 servings

2 pounds <u>frozen</u>, peeled, and
  seeded ½- to 1-inch butternut
  squash cubes

2 cups vegetable or chicken
  broth

2 teaspoons stemmed fresh
  thyme leaves, or 1 teaspoon
  dried thyme

¼ teaspoon grated nutmeg, or
  ⅛ teaspoon ground nutmeg

½ teaspoon table salt

1 cup whole or low-fat milk

½ cup heavy or light cream (but
  not "fat-free" cream)

4 tablespoons (½ stick) butter

2 tablespoons all-purpose flour

Surprisingly light (despite the cream) and quite comforting, this soup is a go-to winter indulgence, especially if you've got a crunchy baguette on hand (or some toast slices). When we were testing these recipes, we kept referring to this soup as "the one that's like melted gelato." That should tell you a lot about its texture.

While you can squirrel fresh butternut squash chunks in the freezer to make this soup, you'll need to make sure those pieces are about 1 inch each. The frozen cubes sold in bags are smaller than the fresh ones from the produce section (and so cook more quickly).

One final note: This soup freezes well in small, individual containers that you can reheat for lunch or dinner.

1. Stir the squash cubes, broth, thyme, nutmeg, and salt in a **6-quart Instant Pot.** Lock the lid onto the pot.

2.

Set the machine for	Set the level for	The valve must be	Set the time for	If necessary, press
PRESSURE COOK	MAX	—	4 minutes with the KEEP WARM setting off	START
SOUP/BROTH, PRESSURE COOK, or MANUAL	HIGH	Closed	5 minutes with the KEEP WARM setting off	START

3. Use the **quick-release method** to bring the pot's pressure back to normal. Unlatch the lid and open the pot. Stir in the milk and cream.

4. Use an immersion blender to puree the soup right in the pot. Or work in halves (or even thirds) to puree the soup in a covered blender. (Remove the knob from the blender's lid and place a towel over the opening so that pressure cannot build up and spew hot soup onto you.) If necessary, return all the soup to the cooker.

5.

Press the button for	Set it for	Set the time for	If necessary, press
SAUTÉ	LOW, LESS, or CUSTOM 250°F	5 minutes	START

6. Bring the soup to a simmer, stirring often. Meanwhile, put the butter in a small, microwave-safe bowl or measuring container and melt it in 5-second increments on high in a microwave. Use a fork to stir in the flour to make a thin paste.

7. When the soup is simmering, whisk (do not stir) the butter mixture into the pot. Continue whisking until the soup is slightly thickened, about 1 minute. Turn off the SAUTÉ function and cool for a couple of minutes before serving.

 Using a **-20°F CHEST FREEZER?** There is no difference in cooking times.

Beyond

- For an **8-quart Instant Pot,** you must use 50 percent more of all the ingredients.

- We kept the herbs simple so the flavor of the soup remains a bit more straightforward. If you want more "herbiness," sprinkle minced fresh parsley or sage leaves on each serving.

- The soup is terrific with crunchy bacon crumbled over each bowlful.

- This soup may well need a grilled cheese sandwich. Here's our favorite recipe: Put about 2 ounces sliced sharp Cheddar between two pieces of whole-wheat or rye bread. Smear a thin coating of regular or low-fat (but not fat-free) mayonnaise on the *outside* of both sides of the sandwich. Lightly coat the inside of a nonstick skillet with nonstick spray, then fry the sandwich over medium heat, turning once, until crisp, 3–4 minutes.

Meatball Minestrone

8 servings

1 pound mini or bite-sized
   meatballs (even vegan and/or
   gluten-free if you like),
   ½ to 1 ounce each

1 quart (4 cups) beef, chicken, or
   vegetable broth

One 28-ounce can diced
   tomatoes packed in juice
   (3½ cups)

One 15-ounce can red kidney
   beans, drained and rinsed
   (1¾ cups)

1 cup <u>frozen</u> chopped onion; or
   1 medium yellow or white
   onion, peeled and chopped

5 ounces (1 cup) <u>frozen</u>
   unseasoned hash brown
   cubes (not frozen shredded
   hash browns)

1 cup dried elbow macaroni or
   gluten-free elbow macaroni
   (the standard mac-and-
   cheese size, not the "large" or
   "giant" elbows)

1 tablespoon stemmed and
   chopped fresh rosemary, or
   2 teaspoons crumbled dried
   rosemary

1 tablespoon stemmed and
   minced fresh oregano leaves,
   or 1½ teaspoons dried
   oregano

½ teaspoon table salt

¼ teaspoon red pepper flakes

¼ teaspoon grated nutmeg, or
   ⅛ teaspoon ground nutmeg

Meatballs, potatoes, beans, macaroni — this soup's got enough in it to make a full meal any weeknight. We can also guarantee it's kid-friendly. We carried the insert of the pot up the hill to our neighbors at the road. (We live in very rural New England so, yes, we have neighbors "at the road.") The boys ate the soup down. You might even consider a second pot's worth if you want some after your boys get done.

You could use any sort of frozen mini meatball for this soup, *as long as* each meatball is ½– 1 ounce in weight. (The size is indicated on the package.) If you have larger frozen meatballs (sometimes called "dinner-size"), add 2 minutes to the timing for either MAX or HIGH pressure.

1. Mix all the ingredients in a **6- or 8-quart Instant Pot.** Lock the lid onto the pot.

2.

Set the machine for	Set the level for	The valve must be	Set the time for	If necessary, press
PRESSURE COOK	MAX	—	10 minutes with the KEEP WARM setting off	START
SOUP/BROTH, PRESSURE COOK, or MANUAL	HIGH	Closed	12 minutes with the KEEP WARM setting off	START

3. Use the **quick-release method** to bring the pot's pressure back to normal. Unlatch the lid and open the pot. Stir well before serving.

Note: For the best gluten-free elbow macaroni (or any gluten-free pasta in the pot, for that matter), look for pasta made with a mix of grains, particularly with corn among the grains. All-rice gluten-free noodles come out of the pot with a texture too slippery for our taste.

Beyond

- Make a vegan soup by using vegetable broth and vegan mini meatballs.

- Add cheese at the end by garnishing each bowl with finely grated Parmigiano-Reggiano.

- Ladle the hot soup over a small mound of baby spinach or kale leaves in each bowl. The soup will wilt the greens in about a minute.

 Using a **–20°F CHEST FREEZER?** There is no difference in cooking times.

Beef and Barley Soup

6–8 servings

1½ quarts (6 cups) beef broth

8 ounces (2 cups) sliced brown or white mushrooms

1 cup raw pearl barley

1 cup frozen chopped onion; or 1 medium yellow or white onion, peeled and chopped

1 cup chopped celery (about 3 stalks)

2 teaspoons stemmed fresh thyme leaves, or 1 teaspoon dried thyme

1 teaspoon stemmed and minced fresh sage leaves, or ½ teaspoon dried sage

½ teaspoon ground allspice

½ teaspoon table salt

½ teaspoon ground black pepper

1 pound frozen ground beef

We tested beef and barley soup with all sorts of meat: frozen bone-in short ribs, frozen flank steak, frozen stew meat. In the end, we learned that a block of frozen ground beef gave us the fastest soup with the least amount of fuss — and a nice beefy flavor, too. Because ground beef thaws before, say, a big flank steak would, it imparts more flavor more quickly.

In other recipes in this book, you break up the frozen ground beef right in the pot after cooking. However, you'll never get bits small enough for the right texture in this soup. (Even with a lot of work, they'll stay slightly larger, a little smaller than mini meatballs.) By shredding the chunk of now-cooked ground beef on a cutting board, you can get it into smaller bits.

1. Mix the broth, mushrooms, barley, onion, celery, thyme, sage, allspice, salt, and pepper in a **6- or 8-quart Instant Pot.** Set the chunk of frozen ground beef in this mixture. Lock the lid onto the pot.

2.

Set the machine for	Set the level for	The valve must be	And set the time for	If necessary, press
PRESSURE COOK	MAX	—	25 minutes with the KEEP WARM setting off	START
SOUP/BROTH, PRESSURE COOK, or MANUAL	HIGH	Closed	30 minutes with the KEEP WARM setting off	START

3. When the machine has finished cooking, turn it off and let its pressure **return to normal naturally,** about 40 minutes.

4. Unlatch the lid and open the pot. Use tongs to transfer the block of beef to a nearby cutting board. Use a large fork and a chef's knife to chop the meat into very small bits, about the size of ground beef crumbles. Stir these back into the soup. If there are any tiny bits of pink in the meat, set the lid askew over the pot and let sit a couple of minutes to continue to cook the meat.

 Using a **-20°F CHEST FREEZER?** There is no difference in cooking times.

Beyond

- For extraordinary flavor, crumble up to 1 ounce dried mushrooms, preferably dried porcinis, into the soup mixture before you add the frozen ground beef.

- For a buttery soup, stir 3 tablespoons unsalted butter, cut into small cubes, into the soup mixture before you add the frozen ground beef.

- Garnish the bowls with a little drizzle of extra-virgin olive oil. Smoked olive oil would be even better! Or garnish the servings with a drizzle of balsamic vinegar.

Pulled Pork Soup

8 servings

8 ounces thin-sliced bacon, chopped

1 cup <u>frozen</u> chopped onion; or 1 medium yellow or white onion, peeled and chopped

2 ounces (½ cup) <u>frozen</u> bell pepper strips; or 1 small green or red bell pepper, stemmed, cored, and thinly sliced

Up to 1 canned chipotle in adobo sauce, stemmed and seeded (see the headnote to the Southwestern Pot Roast on page 134 for more information)

2 tablespoons dark brown sugar

2 tablespoons mild smoked paprika

2 teaspoons ground cumin

1 teaspoon ground dried mustard

1 teaspoon garlic powder

1 teaspoon table salt

One 28-ounce can diced tomatoes packed in juice (3½ cups)

1 quart (4 cups) chicken, beef, or vegetable broth

One 3½-pound <u>frozen</u> boneless pork shoulder or pork butt

How many times have you said this? "Boy, I wish I could turn pulled pork into a soup." Okay, maybe never. But try it once and you'll realize this recipe's a fine way to turn our favorite barbecue dish into a bowl of warm comfort. Grab a boneless pork shoulder or butt for the freezer the next time you see one on sale. In the U.S., the cut often gets marked down right after the big summer holidays: Memorial Day, the Fourth of July, and Labor Day. Take it out of its packaging, removing any extraneous pads or "diapers," then seal it in a plastic bag and freeze for up to 4 months.

Because of possible cross-contamination issues in pork processing, use certified gluten-free bacon, if gluten is a concern in your household.

This recipe makes a lot. Get some containers to freeze the leftovers for a fast meal from the microwave anytime.

1.

Press the button for	Set it for	Set the time for	If necessary, press
SAUTÉ	MEDIUM, NORMAL, or CUSTOM 300°F	10 minutes	START

2. Add the bacon to a **6- or 8-quart Instant Pot.** Cook, stirring occasionally, until browned, about 3 minutes. Stir in the onion, bell pepper, and canned chipotle. Cook, stirring often, until the vegetables are soft and hot, about 4 minutes.

3. Stir in the brown sugar, smoked paprika, cumin, mustard, garlic powder, and salt. Then stir in the tomatoes and broth to scrape up brown bits from the pot's bottom. Turn off the SAUTÉ function and set the pork in the liquid. Lock the lid onto the pot.

4.

Set the machine for	Set the level for	The valve must be	And set the time for	If necessary, press
PRESSURE COOK	MAX	—	1 hour 15 minutes with the KEEP WARM setting off	START
SOUP/BROTH, PRESSURE COOK, or MANUAL	HIGH	Closed	1 hour 30 minutes with the KEEP WARM setting off	START

5. When the machine has finished cooking, turn it off and let its pressure **return to normal naturally,** about 45 minutes.

6. Unlatch the lid and open the cooker. Use a big slotted spoon, a large meat fork, and brute force to transfer the hunk of meat to a nearby cutting board. (Dogs in the kitchen are not helpful. Trust us.) Slice the meat into chunks, discarding any clumps of fat. Chop the meat into small bits, almost threads.

7. Use a large cooking spoon to skim the fat off the surface of the soup and discard. Stir the shredded pork back into the soup, then serve warm.

Note: For all of our Instant Pot recipes that call for them, you *must* use canned tomatoes packed in juice, not in puree. Those packed in puree will make the pot fail. Read the ingredient labels carefully.

Beyond

- Brighten the soup by adding up to 2 teaspoons fresh lime juice with the pork in step 7.

- The salt here is minimal because tastes vary. Pass more at the table.

- There are few vegetables to keep the flavors clean. To make the stew heartier, ladle it over warmed corn kernels in the bowls. Or serve over mashed potatoes.

- The soup is rich. Still, a garnish of shredded Monterey Jack or a Tex-Mex cheese blend would be welcome.

- We also like pickle relish as a garnish..

 Using a **-20°F CHEST FREEZER?** There is no difference in cooking times.

Tortilla Soup

6 servings

One 19-ounce can red enchilada sauce (2¼ cups)

2 cups chicken or vegetable broth

1 teaspoon stemmed fresh thyme leaves, or ½ teaspoon dried thyme

½ teaspoon ground cinnamon

½ teaspoon ground cumin

Six 6-ounce or eight 4-ounce <u>frozen</u> quesadillas or gluten-free quesadillas of any flavor

This recipe seems like a bit of wizardry. By starting with frozen quesadillas, you can transform enchilada sauce and broth into a fast tortilla soup. The recipe works because the filling in those quesadillas (the vegetables, meat, cheese, chiles, and whatever else) falls out and adds body to the soup while the tortillas thicken the enchilada sauce as they expand and thaw. When you open the pot, you'll find the tortillas on top have puffed up. Don't worry — you'll cut them down to smaller bits.

Use either corn or flour quesadillas — and any variety you like. We found this soup worked best with the frozen quesadillas that come two to a 12-ounce package. But in the end, since this dish is a soup, not a stew, there's leeway for the types and sizes of quesadillas you can use.

1.

Press the button for	Set it for	Set the time for	If necessary, press
SAUTÉ	HIGH, MORE, or CUSTOM 400°F	10 minutes	START

2. Stir the enchilada sauce, broth, thyme, cinnamon, and cumin in a **6-quart Instant Pot.** Cook, stirring occasionally, until several wisps of steam come up off the sauce. Add the frozen quesadillas to the sauce without pushing them to the bottom of the pot. (The tops of a couple of the quesadillas will perhaps not be touched by the sauce.) Lock the lid onto the pot.

3.

Set the machine for	Set the level for	The valve must be	And set the time for	If necessary, press
PRESSURE COOK	MAX	—	5 minutes with the KEEP WARM setting off	START
SOUP/ BROTH, PRESSURE COOK, or MANUAL	HIGH	Closed	8 minutes with the KEEP WARM setting off	START

4. Use the **quick-release method** to return the pot's pressure to normal. Unlatch the lid and open the pot. Use cleaned kitchen shears to cut up the quesadillas, or pull them to rough shreds with two forks. Serve the soup by scooping up the broth with bits of the tortillas and their (former) filling.

Beyond

- For an **8-quart Instant Pot,** you must increase the broth to 3 cups.

- For a heartier soup, add one drained and rinsed 15-ounce can of black or red kidney beans or one drained 15-ounce can of corn to the pot after you release the pressure and cut up the quesadillas. Simmer on the SAUTÉ function at MEDIUM, NORMAL, or CUSTOM 300°F for 2–3 minutes, stirring often, just to heat the beans and corn through.

- For a thicker stew, add one of those cans of vegetables mentioned above, plus up to 1 pound chopped, skinned, and deboned rotisserie chicken meat. Simmer in the same way.

Using a **-20°F CHEST FREEZER?** There is no difference in cooking times.

Tater Tot Soup

6–8 servings

1½ quarts (6 cups) chicken or
vegetable broth

2 tablespoons butter

2 teaspoons peeled and minced
garlic

2 teaspoons dried basil,
oregano, or thyme

1 teaspoon onion powder

½ teaspoon ground black pepper

1 pound (3 cups) <u>frozen</u>
unseasoned hash brown
cubes (*not* frozen shredded
hash browns)

1¼ pounds (5 cups) <u>frozen</u> Tater
Tots or potato puffs

8 ounces (2 cups) shredded mild
or sharp Cheddar cheese

Here's the fastest cheese-and-potato soup we can imagine! The Tater Tots break apart — even break down — under pressure, leaving you with little potato shreds, as if you'd grated a potato into the soup. Those potato bits also thicken the soup, particularly as it sits a few minutes after cooking to melt all that (absolutely necessary) cheese. The frozen hash brown cubes then give you more little bits of potato throughout the soup for a better overall texture.

Dried herbs work better than fresh here. They have an earthier flavor that matches the Tater Tots and cheese.

And one other thing: Heat the liquid up before you add the Tater Tots. Otherwise, they fall to the bottom of the pot in the (colder) liquid. You'll end up with a *burn* notice, no question.

1.

Press the button for	Set it for	Set the time for	If necessary, press
SAUTÉ	HIGH, MORE, or CUSTOM 400°F	10 minutes	START

2. Mix the broth, butter, garlic, dried herb, onion powder, and pepper in a **6-quart Instant Pot.** Heat, stirring occasionally, until wisps of steam rise from the liquid. Stir in the hash brown cubes and Tater Tots. Lock the lid onto the pot.

3.

Set the machine for	Set the level for	The valve must be	And set the time for	If necessary, press
PRESSURE COOK	MAX	—	3 minutes with the KEEP WARM setting off	START
SOUP/BROTH, PRESSURE COOK, or MANUAL	HIGH	Closed	4 minutes with the KEEP WARM setting off	START

4. Use the **quick-release method** to bring the pot's pressure back to normal. Unlatch the lid and open the cooker. Stir in the cheese. Set the lid askew over the pot for a couple of minutes until the cheese melts. Stir again, then serve hot.

 Using a **–20°F CHEST FREEZER?** There is no difference in cooking times.

Beyond

- For an **8-quart Instant Pot,** you must increase the broth to 2 quarts (8 cups).

- For a richer soup, stir up to 1 cup heavy or light cream into the soup before you add the cheese in step 4.

- For a sweeter soup, use half regular tots and half sweet potato tots (sometimes called "puffs").

- Garnish the servings with crumbled bacon, sour cream, and/or minced chives (or the green part of a scallion). Or crisp Tater Tots in a skillet, toaster oven, or an air fryer and use them as a garnish on the soup.

Lasagna Soup

6 servings

One 28-ounce can diced
tomatoes packed in juice
(3½ cups)

2 cups chicken or vegetable
broth

1 pound <u>frozen</u> ground beef

One 24-ounce jar plain marinara
sauce (3 cups)

1 pound (4 to 5 cups) <u>frozen</u>
chopped mixed vegetables
(*not* a stir-fry blend)

1 tablespoon dried Italian
seasoning blend

½ teaspoon table salt, optional
(check to see if the seasoning
blend includes salt)

8 regular dried lasagna noodles
(*not* no-boil noodles)

Grated mozzarella cheese, for
garnish

We've seen plenty of internet recipes for lasagna soup. What's the deal with ziti or fusilli in the mix? Lasagna has to have lasagna noodles! By breaking up dried noodles and cooking them in the soup, we can get the taste and texture of lasagna in every bowl.

For the best results, the broken bits of the lasagna noodles should be fairly small, maybe 2 or 3 inches long. You want a piece to hang off (but not slip off) a spoonful of soup. Break the noodles right over the pot so that any shards fall in as well.

The frozen ground beef is set on a rack to help its texture. If it sits directly in the liquid, it can get overcooked and a bit tough. This way, the meat steams before it actually gets into the sauce. It may be pink (or even red) inside after the first cooking. It will continue to cook in the second pressure step.

1. Set a colander or a fine-mesh sieve over a **6- or 8-quart Instant Pot** (with its stainless-steel insert in place, of course). Drain the tomatoes in the colander or sieve, letting the liquid fall into the pot below. Remove the colander or sieve and reserve the drained tomato pieces. Stir the broth into the pot. Set the pot's rack (with the handles up) or a large, open vegetable steamer inside the pot. Set the chunk of ground beef on the rack or in the steamer. Lock the lid onto the pot.

2.

Set the machine for	Set the level for	The valve must be	And set the time for	If necessary, press
PRESSURE COOK	MAX	—	18 minutes with the KEEP WARM setting off	START
SOUP/ BROTH, PRESSURE COOK, or MANUAL	HIGH	Closed	20 minutes with the KEEP WARM setting off	START

3. Use the **quick-release method** to bring the pot's pressure back to normal. Unlatch the lid and open the cooker. Use tongs or silicone cooking mitts to remove the rack or steamer from the cooker, letting the block of ground beef fall into the sauce. Use the edge of a large cooking spoon and a meat fork to break the ground beef into small, bite-sized chunks — not threads, but like very small meatballs.

4. Stir in the reserved drained tomatoes, the marinara sauce, vegetables, dried seasoning blend, and salt (if using). Break each of the noodles into six to eight pieces over the pot. Stir well, then lock the lid back onto the pot.

5.

Set the machine for	Set the level for	The valve must be	And set the time for	If necessary, press
PRESSURE COOK	MAX	—	5 minutes with the KEEP WARM setting off	START
SOUP/ BROTH, PRESSURE COOK, or MANUAL	HIGH	Closed	6 minutes with the KEEP WARM setting off	START

6. Use the **quick-release method** to bring the pot's pressure back to normal. Unlatch the lid and open the pot. Serve by the bowlful with lots of cheese sprinkled over each.

 Using a **-20°F CHEST FREEZER?** There is no difference in cooking times.

Beyond

- Serve the soup over little mounds of ricotta.

- Garnish the soup with stemmed and minced fresh oregano, parsley, and/or thyme leaves.

- And/or garnish each serving with extra-virgin olive oil.

Chinese Dumpling Soup

6 servings

2½ quarts (10 cups) chicken or
vegetable broth

4 medium scallions, trimmed
and thinly sliced

One ½-inch-thick slice of deli
smoked ham (2 to 3 ounces),
any rind removed, the meat
sliced into matchsticks

2 tablespoons regular or
reduced-sodium soy sauce or
tamari

½ teaspoon ground dried ginger

Two 12-ounce boxes frozen
chicken, pork, or vegetable
Chinese dumplings, stuffed
wontons, or pot stickers (10 to
12 per box)

Here's an absurdly easy version of wonton soup—the Chinese take-out
classic—and a quick meal when you want to make a mad dash to the TV
after work to stream the latest. Unlike the quesadillas in the Tortilla Soup
(pages 34–35), the wontons or pot stickers don't fall apart so easily. Of
course, a few may come undone. They just add a little more body and
flavor to the broth.

1.

Press the button for	Set it for	Set the time for	If necessary, press
SAUTÉ	HIGH, MORE, or CUSTOM 400°F	10 minutes	START

2. Stir the broth, scallions, ham, soy sauce or tamari, and ginger in a **6- or
8-quart Instant Pot.** Cook, stirring occasionally, until many wisps of
steam rise from the mixture. Stir in the frozen dumplings. Turn off the
SAUTÉ function and lock the lid onto the pot.

3.

Set the machine for	Set the level for	The valve must be	And set the time for	If necessary, press
PRESSURE COOK	MAX	—	3 minutes with the KEEP WARM setting off	START
SOUP/BROTH, PRESSURE COOK, or MANUAL	HIGH	Closed	4 minutes with the KEEP WARM setting off	START

4. Use the **quick-release method** to bring the pot's pressure back to normal. Unlatch the lid and open the pot. Stir well before serving.

Beyond

- For a more complex flavor, substitute five-spice powder for the ground dried ginger.

- For a more gingery flavor, add up to 1 tablespoon peeled and minced fresh ginger with the soup ingredients.

- For a more savory flavor, add up to 1 sheet kombu (a dried seaweed) with the soup ingredients. Remove the kombu before serving.

- For more heft, stir 2 cups stemmed, washed, and shredded baby bok choy or bagged shredded Brussels sprouts into the soup when you open the pot in step 4. Simmer on the SAUTÉ setting at MEDIUM, NORMAL, or CUSTOM 300°F for 1–2 minutes to wilt the vegetable before serving.

- Garnish the servings with *sambal oelek* or another chunky red chile sauce, if desired.

Using a **-20°F CHEST FREEZER?** There is no difference in cooking times.

Creamy Cod Chowder

4–6 servings

3 cups chicken or vegetable broth

8 ounces (1½ cups) frozen unseasoned hash brown cubes (*not* frozen shredded hash browns)

8 ounces (1½ cups) frozen corn kernels; or the fresh kernels cut off 2 husked medium ears of corn

1 cup frozen chopped onion; or 1 medium yellow or white onion, peeled and chopped

2 teaspoons stemmed and minced fresh sage leaves, or 1 teaspoon dried sage

½ teaspoon celery seeds

1 bay leaf

½ teaspoon table salt, optional

Four 6-ounce or two 12-ounce frozen cod fillets (that is, 1½ pounds)

1 cup regular or low-fat evaporated milk (*not* fat-free)

2 tablespoons cornstarch

Here's a freezer-to-pot version of the classic, creamy chowder, a favorite across New England. Although the hash brown cubes will "melt" a bit at the edges and thicken the soup, it still needs a cornstarch slurry to give it the right texture.

The salt is optional because fish fillets — particularly frozen ones that may have been coated in various preservatives — are notoriously salty. Pass crunchy sea salt at the table instead.

1. Mix the broth, hash brown cubes, corn, onion, sage, celery seeds, bay leaf, and salt (if using) in a **6-quart Instant Pot.** Nestle the cod fillets into this mixture, then lock the lid onto the pot.

2.

Set the machine for	Set the level for	The valve must be	And set the time for	If necessary, press
PRESSURE COOK	MAX	—	4 minutes with the KEEP WARM setting off	START
SOUP/BROTH, PRESSURE COOK, or MANUAL	HIGH	CLOSED	5 minutes with the KEEP WARM setting off	START

3. When the machine has finished cooking, turn it off and let its pressure **return to normal naturally** for 10 minutes. Then use the **quick-release method** to get rid of any residual pressure in the pot.

4. Whisk the evaporated milk and cornstarch in a small bowl until smooth. Unlatch the lid and open the pot.

5.

Press the button for	Set it for	Set the time for	If necessary, press
SAUTÉ	MEDIUM, NORMAL, or CUSTOM 300°F	10 minutes	START

6. Bring the soup to a simmer, stirring gently to break the cod fillets into small pieces. Stir in the milk mixture and continue stirring until bubbling and thickened, 1–2 minutes. Turn off the SAUTÉ function, remove the bay leaf, and serve hot.

Beyond

- For an **8-quart Instant Pot,** you must increase all the ingredients by 50 percent.

- For a richer finish, float a pat of butter on each serving.

- For an even richer dish, stir ¼ cup heavy or light cream into the soup with the evaporated-milk mixture.

- For a brinier soup, use 1½ cups chicken or vegetable broth and 1½ cups fish stock or bottled clam juice. In this case, omit the salt.

- For more heat, add up to 1 teaspoon red pepper flakes with the sage and celery seed.

- Serve the soup over crusty croutons — or even stale slices of bread that have been toasted until golden brown.

❄ Using a **-20°F CHEST FREEZER?** There is no difference in cooking times.

Manhattan Fish Chowder

6 servings

1 quart (4 cups) chicken or vegetable broth

One 14-ounce can diced tomatoes packed in juice (1⅔ cups)

1 cup dry white or dry rosé wine

5 ounces (1 cup) <u>frozen</u> unseasoned hash brown cubes (*not* frozen shredded hash browns)

1 cup <u>frozen</u> chopped onion; or 1 medium yellow or white onion, peeled and chopped

2 tablespoons tomato paste

2 tablespoons stemmed and minced fresh basil leaves

1 tablespoon stemmed and minced fresh oregano leaves, or 2 teaspoons dried oregano

Up to 1 tablespoon peeled and minced garlic

2 bay leaves

½ teaspoon table salt

1 pound <u>frozen</u> skinless white-fleshed fish fillets, such as halibut, cod, or mahi-mahi

½ pound <u>frozen</u> peeled and deveined raw medium shrimp (30–35 per pound)

½ pound <u>frozen</u> bay scallops

This version of chowder has no cream — and has never been easier to cook, thanks to the way the pot can cook frozen fish fillets and frozen shellfish. The pressure extracts lots of flavor from the frozen seafood as it thaws, rendering the meal a chowder lover's dream. Although many people like oyster crackers with this, we're partial to old-fashioned saltines.

1. Mix the broth, tomatoes, wine, hash brown cubes, onion, tomato paste, basil, oregano, garlic, bay leaves, and salt in a **6- or 8-quart Instant Pot.** Nestle the fish, shrimp, and scallops into this mixture, then lock the lid onto the pot.

2.

Set the machine for	Set the level for	The valve must be	And set the time for	If necessary, press
PRESSURE COOK	MAX	—	4 minutes with the KEEP WARM setting off	START
SOUP/BROTH, PRESSURE COOK, or MANUAL	HIGH	Closed	5 minutes with the KEEP WARM setting off	START

3. When the machine has finished cooking, turn it off and let its pressure **return to normal naturally** for 10 minutes. Then use the **quick-release method** to get rid of any residual pressure in the pot. Unlatch the lid and open the pot. Stir the soup gently to break the fish fillets into chunks. Set aside with the lid askew over the cooker for a couple of minutes to blend the flavors.

Beyond

- If you don't want to use wine in the soup, substitute tomato juice.

- For heat, add up to 1 tablespoon red pepper flakes with the herbs and spices.

- For more heft, add up to 1 cup frozen lima beans with the other frozen vegetables.

- Or add up to 1 cup trimmed and chopped fresh green beans to the soup after cooking but before setting it aside for a few minutes covered.

- For a treat, toast 1-inch-thick French or Italian bread rounds on a baking sheet under the broiler, turning once, until golden brown on both sides. Lightly butter one side of each round, then set a few in each bowl and ladle the soup on top.

 Using a **-20°F CHEST FREEZER?** There is no difference in cooking times.

2
Noodles

Properly cooked pasta—that is, *al dente*, with just a little resistance (or chew) in each bite—is a goal that eludes many an Instant Pot user. But it's easy to get great results if you follow a few rules, as we'll show you.

In many of these recipes the pasta is not frozen (although we do use frozen ravioli and frozen tortellini). But the meat or seafood and vegetables are icy stuff. Getting those items thawed and cooked at the same time as cooking dried pasta would result in mushy, overcooked noodles. That's why a lot of these recipes take two steps—that is, the frozen fare is thawed and cooked under pressure; then the pot is opened, the pasta is added, and the whole thing goes under pressure again. We want to make sure the pasta doesn't get squishy.

We always call for dried pasta (except with the recipes that use frozen stuffed pasta, of course). Fresh pasta can be temperamental, even on the stovetop. Besides, we felt that dried noodles were more in keeping with the spirit of this book about pantry (and freezer) cooking.

And one more general rule before you get started: When we say to warm the liquid in the pot until steaming, we mean it. Go beyond the first little wisp of steam. The liquid needs to be warm to protect the pasta. That's the real secret to perfect noodle dishes that start with frozen ingredients.

Road Map: **Ravioli**

4–6 servings

3 cups water; or 2½ cups water plus ½ cup broth of any type, wine of any type, or dry vermouth

Two 13-ounce bags <u>frozen</u> standard-size meat or cheese ravioli (not mini ravioli)

Here are a few of the problems with frozen stuffed pasta in the pot: Some types, like manicotti or stuffed shells, are open on the ends, so the filling falls out as they thaw and cook under pressure. Others, like frozen tortellini, are so small that they bobble around in water, broth, or wine, some eventually ending up on the pot's bottom and sticking. (However, frozen tortellini will work in a thicker sauce — see pages 68–69.)

Frozen ravioli, however, are easier. Here's the trick: Get the water (or liquid you choose) heated up before you dump them in. The water (or liquid) doesn't need to be simmering, just good and hot. Not only does this prevent the ravioli from sticking to the pot's bottom, it also ensures they don't clump together as they cook.

This road-map recipe offers you a basic way to cook the frozen ravioli. Then several ways to customize the ravioli follow. In other words, there are lots of choices!

1.

Press the button for	Set it for	Set the time for	If necessary, press
SAUTÉ	HIGH, MORE, or CUSTOM 400°F	10 minutes	START

2. Pour the water or water and other liquid combination into a **6- or 8-quart Instant Pot.** Heat until many wisps of steams rise off the liquid. (The mixture does not need to be simmering.) Pour in the ravioli and stir well. Turn off the SAUTÉ function and lock the lid onto the pot.

3.

Set the machine for	Set the level for	The valve must be	And set the time for	If necessary, press
PRESSURE COOK	MAX	—	3 minutes with the KEEP WARM setting off	START
SOUP/BROTH, PRESSURE COOK, or MANUAL	HIGH	Closed	5 minutes with the KEEP WARM setting off	START

4. Use the **quick-release method** to bring the pot's pressure back to normal. Use silicone cooking mitts, thick hot pads, or an insert holder (a specialty tool for an Instant Pot) to pick up the (hot!) insert and drain the ravioli in a colander set in the sink.

5. Then choose how to finish the dish…

- Toss the cooked ravioli in a bowl with a 24-ounce jar (3 cups) of marinara or spaghetti sauce. Spread everything in a 9 x 13-inch baking dish and cover with up to 8 ounces (2 cups) shredded mozzarella. Bake uncovered in a 350°F oven for 20 minutes, until bubbling and lightly browned.

- Mix the hot ravioli with up to 1 to 1½ cups purchased pesto. Spoon onto serving plates and top with finely grated Parmigiano-Reggiano and/or red pepper flakes.

- For an easy sauce, melt 8 tablespoons (1 stick) butter in the insert (after you've taken out the ravioli), using the pot's SAUTÉ function on MEDIUM, NORMAL, or CUSTOM 300°F. Add ½ cup chopped walnuts, chopped pecans, or whole pine nuts, then stir until the nuts just begin to brown, about 2 minutes. Turn off the SAUTÉ function and remove the (hot!) insert from the pot. Pour the butter and nuts over the ravioli, toss well, and season with ground black pepper or red pepper flakes.

- Cool the ravioli completely in the colander, then add to lots of chopped, crunchy vegetables (such as celery, carrots, red onion, sugar snap peas, broccoli florets, cauliflower florets, or trimmed green beans). Add as much creamy Italian dressing as you like for a tasty new take on pasta salad.

 Using a **–20°F CHEST FREEZER?** There is no difference in cooking times.

Spaghetti and Meatballs

4 servings

One 24-ounce jar any style
marinara, red spaghetti
sauce, or red pasta sauce
(3 cups)

3 cups chicken or vegetable
broth

1½ pounds <u>frozen</u> mini or
bite-sized meatballs (even
vegan and/or gluten-free if
that's a concern), ½ to 1
ounce each

12 ounces dried regular
spaghetti or gluten-free
spaghetti

Here's how to use frozen meatballs to make a tasty spaghetti supper any
weeknight. We've left the dish pretty simple. See the suggestions in the
Beyond section for ways to gussy it up.

But one warning: Do not use a creamy pasta sauce (like a four-cheese
sauce or a bottled vodka sauce) because the cream can break under
pressure.

1.

Press the button for	Set it for	Set the time for	If necessary, press
SAUTÉ	HIGH, MORE, or CUSTOM 400°F	10 minutes	START

2. Stir the spaghetti sauce and broth in a **6- or 8-quart Instant Pot.** Stir in
the meatballs. When many wisps of steam start to rise from the liquid,
turn off the SAUTÉ function and stir everything well.

3. Break the pasta in half. Lay half of it in one direction on top of the
sauce; lay the other half at a 90-degree angle. Press gently to immerse the
pasta partially in the sauce. Lock the lid onto the pot.

4.

Set the machine for	Set the level for	The valve must be	And set the time for	If necessary, press
PRESSURE COOK	MAX	—	5 minutes with the KEEP WARM setting off	START
MEAT/STEW, PRESSURE COOK, or MANUAL	HIGH	Closed	6 minutes with the KEEP WARM setting off	START

5. Use the **quick-release method** to bring the pot's pressure back to normal. Unlatch the lid and open the pot. Stir gently to mix the pasta into the sauce. Set the lid askew over the pot and let sit for a couple of minutes to allow the pasta to absorb more of the sauce. Serve in bowls.

Beyond

- Ladle the spaghetti and meatballs over small scoops of ricotta in the serving bowls.

- Garnish the servings with stemmed and minced fresh herbs (particularly oregano, rosemary, parsley, and/or thyme).

- And/or garnish with finely grated Parmigiano-Reggiano.

- For a richer flavor, use 2½ cups broth plus ½ cup red wine.

- Or add up to 4 tablespoons (½ stick) butter to the pot with the dried spaghetti.

 Using a **-20°F CHEST FREEZER?** There is no difference in cooking times.

Cheesy Chili Mac

4 servings

One 28-ounce can diced
  tomatoes packed in juice
  (3½ cups)

1 cup unsweetened apple cider,
  hard cider, or beer of any sort
  (a porter tastes best!)

1 pound <u>frozen</u> ground beef

10 ounces dried ziti or
  gluten-free dried ziti

One 15-ounce can beans of any
  variety, drained and rinsed
  (1¾ cups)

¼ cup standard chili powder

1 teaspoon dried oregano

1 teaspoon ground cumin

½ teaspoon table salt

8 ounces shredded Cheddar,
  Swiss, or Monterey Jack
  cheese, or a Tex-Mex blend

It's hard to beat a pot of chili mac. It's even harder to beat it when you don't have to remember to thaw the ground beef! If you haven't taken the meat out of its container and diaper before freezing it, there are a few tricks on page 5 for getting the job done.

Note that the chili powder used is the standard, American variety, not a "pure" chili powder made with only one type of chile (like chipotle or ancho). And remember: Chili powder loses its oomph after a year or so on the shelf. Consider replacing yours if you inherited it from your great aunt's cupboard.

1. Mix the tomatoes and cider or beer in a **6- or 8-quart Instant Pot.** Add the block of frozen ground beef, partially submerging it in the liquid. Lock the lid onto the pot.

2.

Set the machine for	Set the level for	The valve must be	And set the time for	If necessary, press
PRESSURE COOK	MAX	—	12 minutes with the KEEP WARM setting off	START
MEAT/STEW, PRESSURE COOK, or MANUAL	HIGH	Closed	15 minutes with the KEEP WARM setting off	START

3. Use the **quick-release method** to bring the pot's pressure back to normal. Unlatch the lid and open the cooker. Use the edge of a large metal spoon and a meat fork to break the clump of meat into small chunks, a little smaller than mini meatballs. (The meat will still be pink or even red in the middle.) Stir in the ziti, beans, chili powder, oregano, cumin, and salt until the pasta is partially submerged or lightly coated in the sauce. Lock the lid back onto the pot.

4.

Set the machine for	Set the level for	The valve must be	And set the time for	If necessary, press
PRESSURE COOK	MAX	—	5 minutes with the KEEP WARM setting off	START
MEAT/STEW, PRESSURE COOK, or MANUAL	HIGH	Closed	6 minutes with the KEEP WARM setting off	START

5. Use the **quick-release method** to bring the pot's pressure back to normal. Unlatch the lid and open the cooker. Stir in the cheese, then set the lid askew over the pot and let sit for a couple of minutes to melt the cheese. Stir well before serving.

Beyond

- Add up to 1 cup frozen chopped onion, frozen corn kernels, or frozen bell pepper strips with the pasta.

- Serve with jarred pickled jalapeño rings and sour cream. Or go all out and scatter both pickle relish *and* pickled jalapeño rings on top of the sour cream. (Trust us.)

 Using a **-20°F CHEST FREEZER?** There is no difference in cooking times.

Mac and Cheese and Meatballs

4 servings

1 quart (4 cups) chicken or
vegetable broth

1 pound mini or bite-sized
<u>frozen</u> turkey meatballs (even
vegan and/or gluten-free
meatballs, if that's a concern),
½ to 1 ounce each

4 tablespoons (½ stick) butter

2 teaspoons stemmed fresh
thyme leaves, or 1 teaspoon
dried thyme

1 teaspoon onion powder

1 teaspoon garlic powder

½ teaspoon table salt

16 ounces elbow macaroni or
gluten-free elbow macaroni
(*not* "giant" or "jumbo"
macaroni)

12 ounces (3 cups) shredded
Cheddar, Swiss, mozzarella,
Havarti, Monterey Jack, or
other semi-firm cheese, or
even a blend of cheeses

1 ounce (½ cup) finely grated
Parmigiano-Reggiano

½ cup heavy or light cream
(but *not* "fat-free")

This one's an entire comfort-food casserole in one pot! The dish is a pretty standard mac and cheese, combined with meatballs — a fusion of two favorite comfort foods in every serving.

You can use frozen beef or pork mini meatballs (so long as they are ½–1 ounce each). However, we found that turkey meatballs have a milder flavor, so the dish tasted more like cheese than meat — that is, more the way a mac and cheese should taste.

1.

Press the button for	Set it for	Set the time for	If necessary, press
SAUTÉ	HIGH, MORE, or CUSTOM 400°F	10 minutes	START

2. Mix the broth, meatballs, butter, thyme, onion powder, garlic powder, and salt in a **6- or 8-quart Instant Pot.** Heat until many wisps of steam rise from the liquid. Turn off the SAUTÉ function. Stir in the macaroni and lock the lid onto the pot.

3.

Set the machine for	Set the level for	The valve must be	And set the time for	If necessary, press
PRESSURE COOK	MAX	—	5 minutes with the KEEP WARM setting off	START
MEAT/STEW, PRESSURE COOK, or MANUAL	HIGH	Closed	6 minutes with the KEEP WARM setting off	START

4. Use the **quick-release method** to bring the pot's pressure back to normal. Unlatch the lid and open the cooker.

5.

Press the button for	Set it for	Set the time for	If necessary, press
SAUTÉ	MEDIUM, NORMAL, or CUSTOM 400°F	5 minutes	START

6. Stir in the shredded cheese, grated Parmesan, and cream until the cheese is melted and bubbly. Turn off the SAUTÉ function; set the lid askew over the pot and let sit for a couple of minutes. Serve warm.

Beyond

- For more heft, stir in up to 2 cups packed baby spinach or kale at the same time as the cheese and cream.

- Garnish the servings with minced chives, stemmed and minced fresh parsley leaves, ground black pepper, grated nutmeg, and/or red pepper flakes.

 Using a **-20°F CHEST FREEZER?** There is no difference in cooking times.

Ground Beef and Noodle Goulash

4–6 servings

One 28-ounce can diced tomatoes packed in juice (3½ cups)

2 cups beef or chicken broth

2 whole jarred roasted red peppers, cut into thin strips

1 tablespoon mild paprika

2 teaspoons stemmed and minced fresh oregano leaves or 1 teaspoon dried oregano

½ teaspoon fennel seeds

½ teaspoon table salt

1 pound <u>frozen</u> ground beef

12 ounces regular, no-yolk, or gluten-free dried egg noodles

Although there's nothing authentically Hungarian about this dish, it's a reasonable replication of the dish called goulash that was a favorite in the '50s and '60s in North America, often served at roadside diners. Once the ground beef's been cooked, chop it into small chunks (instead of shreds) so the dish is more like a casserole rather than a stew.

There's nothing like good paprika. It has a peppery flavor and isn't just a red coloring agent. You need not (and probably shouldn't) use "hot" Hungarian paprika here, but a better bottling of ground paprika will make all the difference. If your paprika is more than a year or so old, trade up!

1. Stir the tomatoes, broth, red pepper strips, paprika, oregano, fennel seeds, and salt in a **6- or 8-quart Instant Pot.** Set the chunk of ground beef into this sauce. Lock the lid onto the pot.

2.

Set the machine for	Set the level for	The valve must be	And set the time for	If necessary, press
PRESSURE COOK	MAX	—	12 minutes with the KEEP WARM setting off	START
MEAT/STEW, PRESSURE COOK, or MANUAL	HIGH	Closed	15 minutes with the KEEP WARM setting off	START

3. Use the **quick-release method** to bring the pot's pressure back to normal. Unlatch the lid and open the cooker. Use the edge of a large metal spoon and a meat fork to break the ground beef chunk into small, bite-sized bits, about like tiny meatballs. (The meat will still be pink or red inside.) Stir in the egg noodles and lock the lid back onto the pot.

4.

Set the machine for	Set the level for	The valve must be	And set the time for	If necessary, press
PRESSURE COOK	MAX		3 minutes with the KEEP WARM setting off	START
MEAT/STEW, PRESSURE COOK, or MANUAL	HIGH	Closed	4 minutes with the KEEP WARM setting off	START

5. Use the **quick-release method** again to bring the pot's pressure back to normal. Unlatch the lid and open the cooker. Stir well before serving.

Using a **−20°F CHEST FREEZER?** There is no difference in cooking times.

Beyond

- For a richer stew, stir up to ½ cup heavy or light cream into the goulash after opening the cooker in step 5.

- Or for brighter flavor, stir up to 1 tablespoon balsamic vinegar into the goulash after opening the cooker in step 5. (But do not use both cream and vinegar — the cream will curdle.)

- Add up to 2 cups frozen mixed vegetables: Scatter them over the top of the dish after you stir in the noodles in step 3. (That way, they'll steam on top of the dish without dropping the temperature of the sauce too much.

- Garnish the servings with ground black or red pepper, if desired.

All-American Chop Suey

4–6 servings

One 28-ounce can diced tomatoes packed in juice (3½ cups)

2 cups beef or chicken broth

½ cup <u>frozen</u> chopped onion; or 1 small yellow or white onion, peeled and chopped

2 teaspoons onion powder

1 teaspoon mild paprika

1 teaspoon garlic powder

½ teaspoon ground cinnamon

Up to ½ teaspoon red pepper flakes

½ teaspoon table salt

1 pound <u>frozen</u> ground beef

12 ounces elbow or gluten-free elbow macaroni (*not* "giant" or "jumbo" macaroni)

4 ounces (1 cup) <u>frozen</u> chopped bell pepper; or 1 medium red or green bell pepper, stemmed, cored, and chopped

This is not a Chinese dish — or even an American take on a Chinese dish. Instead, it's a New England pasta casserole that was something of a mid-century dinner-time staple. American "chop suey" probably got its name because everything was chopped up and mixed together.

The key to the flavor is the blend of paprika and cinnamon. The dish is still popular in upper New England, especially in Maine at small diners. We think it deserves a comeback for its comfort-food flair. (For Chinatown-Style Chop Suey, see pages 102–103.)

1. Mix the tomatoes, broth, onion, onion powder, paprika, garlic powder, cinnamon, red pepper flakes, and salt in a **6- or 8-quart Instant Pot.** Set the chunk of ground beef in this sauce. Lock the lid onto the pot.

2.

Set the machine for	Set the level for	The valve must be	And set the time for	If necessary, press
PRESSURE COOK	MAX	—	12 minutes with the KEEP WARM setting off	START
MEAT/STEW, PRESSURE COOK, or MANUAL	HIGH	Closed	15 minutes with the KEEP WARM setting off	START

3. Use the **quick-release method** to bring the pot's pressure back to normal. Unlatch the lid and open the pot. Use the edge of a large metal spoon and a meat fork to break the ground beef into bite-sized bits, smaller than mini meatballs. Stir in the macaroni and bell pepper. Lock the lid back onto the pot.

4.

Set the machine for	Set the level for	The valve must be	And set the time for	If necessary, press
PRESSURE COOK	MAX	—	5 minutes with the KEEP WARM setting off	START
MEAT/STEW, PRESSURE COOK, or MANUAL	HIGH	Closed	6 minutes with the KEEP WARM setting off	START

5. Use the **quick-release method** again to bring the pot's pressure back to normal. Unlatch the lid and open the cooker. Stir well before serving.

 Using a **–20°F CHEST FREEZER?** There is no difference in cooking times.

Beyond

- Skew this dish toward the flavors of moussaka by using frozen ground lamb instead of beef and stirring up to 2 cups peeled and diced fresh eggplant in with the bell pepper.

- For a slightly sweeter dish, use 1½ cups broth plus ½ cup dry red wine (such as zinfandel).

- If you really want to pretend you're at a Maine diner, top each serving with a fried egg.

Ground Beef Lo Mein

4 servings

2 cups chicken broth

¼ cup regular or reduced-sodium soy sauce or tamari

2 tablespoons ketchup

1 tablespoon unseasoned rice vinegar (see headnote on page 92); or 2 teaspoons apple cider vinegar

Up to 1 tablespoon hot red pepper sauce, preferably sriracha

½ teaspoon ground dried ginger

1 pound frozen ground beef

1 pound (4 to 5 cups) frozen chopped vegetables for stir-fry (discard any seasoning packet)

8 ounces dried spaghetti or dried gluten-free spaghetti

This dish is another fast way to get a version of a take-out classic on the table with frozen ground beef in the mix. Unfortunately, fresh Chinese lo mein noodles will not work. And dried Chinese egg noodles cook much more quickly than standard pasta, and so turn too soggy. We opt for standard pasta for *both* convenience and texture.

1. Mix the broth, soy sauce or tamari, ketchup, vinegar, hot sauce, and ginger in a **6-quart Instant Pot.** Set the chunk of ground beef into this sauce. Lock the lid onto the pot.

2.

Set the machine for	Set the level for	The valve must be	And set the time for	If necessary, press
PRESSURE COOK	MAX	—	12 minutes with the KEEP WARM setting off	START
MEAT/STEW, PRESSURE COOK, or MANUAL	HIGH	Closed	15 minutes with the KEEP WARM setting off	START

3. Use the **quick-release method** to bring the pot's pressure back to normal. Unlatch the lid and open the cooker. Use the edge of a large metal spoon and a meat fork to break the ground beef into bite-sized bits, each about the size of a mini meatball, maybe some (or lots) even smaller. (The ground beef may still be pink or even red inside.)

4. Stir in the vegetables. Break the spaghetti in half. Lay half the noodles on top of the sauce in one direction; lay the other half at a 90-degree angle on top. Use a spoon to press the pasta gently down into the sauce, just so most of it is smeared with a little sauce. Lock the lid back onto the pot.

5.

Set the machine for	Set the level for	The valve must be	And set the time for	If necessary, press
PRESSURE COOK	MAX	—	5 minutes with the KEEP WARM setting off	START
MEAT/STEW, PRESSURE COOK, or MANUAL	HIGH	Closed	6 minutes with the KEEP WARM setting off	START

6. Use the **quick-release method** again to bring the pot's pressure back to normal. Unlatch the lid and open the cooker. Stir well. Set the lid over the pot and set aside for a few minutes to let the pasta absorb some of the excess liquid. Serve warm.

 Using a **-20°F CHEST FREEZER?** There is no difference in cooking times.

Beyond

- For an **8-quart Instant Pot,** you must increase all the ingredients except for the ground beef by 50 percent. (You *can* indeed use 1½ pounds frozen ground beef, although finding a half pound of frozen ground beef can be difficult.)

- For a (somewhat) more authentic flavor, substitute hoisin sauce for the ketchup and/or use Chinese black vinegar instead of the rice or apple cider vinegar.

- For more gingery pop, omit the ground dried ginger and use up to 1 tablespoon peeled and minced fresh ginger.

Beef and Noodle Stroganoff

4–6 servings

3 cups beef or chicken broth

½ cup <u>frozen</u> chopped onion; or
   1 small yellow or white onion,
   peeled and chopped

4 tablespoons (½ stick) butter

2 teaspoons mild paprika

½ teaspoon dried sage

½ teaspoon onion powder

½ teaspoon table salt

½ teaspoon ground black pepper

One 9-ounce box <u>frozen</u>
   Steak-umm sliced steaks,
   each sheet broken into four or
   five pieces

12 ounces regular, no-yolk, or
   gluten-free dried egg noodles

½ cup whole or low-fat milk

1 tablespoon all-purpose flour

½ cup regular or low-fat sour
   cream

Well, okay, not *true* stroganoff. But here's a quick rendition of the American version of this classic braise, this time made with Steak-umm steak slices, a freezer classic. This saucy casserole is actually a cross between stroganoff (with the sour cream but without the mushrooms) and paprikash (with all that paprika in it). It'll be a bit wet when you open the pot in step 4. No worries: The pasta and the flour slurry will thicken it all up.

Steak-umms are usually sold in three to five flat strips per box, each strip separated by a sheet of wax or parchment paper. The meat strips are so thin that they're easy to break into four or five pieces each, even when frozen.

1.

Press the button for	Set it for	Set the time for	If necessary, press
SAUTÉ	HIGH, MORE, or CUSTOM 400°F	10 minutes	START

2. Mix the broth, onion, butter, paprika, sage, onion powder, salt, and pepper in a **6- or 8-quart Instant Pot.** Cook, stirring occasionally, until the butter melts and many wisps of steam come off the liquid. Turn off the SAUTÉ function; stir in the Steak-umms and the noodles. Lock the lid onto the pot.

3.

Set the machine for	Set the level for	The valve must be	And set the time for	If necessary, press
PRESSURE COOK	MAX	—	3 minutes with the KEEP WARM setting off	START
MEAT/STEW, PRESSURE COOK, or MANUAL	HIGH	Closed	4 minutes with the KEEP WARM setting off	START

4. Use the **quick-release method** to bring the pot's pressure back to normal. Unlatch the lid and open the cooker.

5.

Press the button for	Set it for	Set the time for	If necessary, press
SAUTÉ	HIGH, MORE, or CUSTOM 400°F	5 minutes	START

6. As the dish comes to a simmer, whisk the milk and flour in a small bowl until smooth. Whisk this slurry into the pot in a slow stream. Cook, whisking often, until the sauce is thickened, less than 1 minute. Turn off the SAUTÉ function and let the sauce stop bubbling. Stir in the sour cream until uniform, then serve.

Beyond

- Add up to 1 cup frozen peas (or frozen peas and carrots) to the dish. Scatter them over the top of the dish after stirring in the meat and pasta in step 2.

- For a spicy dish, substitute up to 2 teaspoons hot Hungarian paprika for the mild paprika. Or add 1 teaspoon hot paprika to the existing 2 teaspoons mild paprika.

 Using a **-20°F CHEST FREEZER?** There is no difference in cooking times.

Ziti with Sausage and Peppers

4–6 servings

1 pound <u>frozen</u> hot or mild Italian sausage (pork or turkey; gluten-free, if that is a concern), cut into 1-inch pieces

One 24-ounce jar plain marinara or spaghetti sauce (3 cups)

2 cups chicken broth

1 tablespoon dried Italian seasoning blend

1 pound (4 cups) <u>frozen</u> bell pepper strips (any color)

12 ounces dried ziti or gluten-free dried ziti

6 ounces (1½ cups) shredded mozzarella cheese

The best sausage for this sort of easy pasta casserole are the fat links that come five or six to a package. (Or, of course, honest-to-God Italian sausages from an Italian butcher. But who would freeze those instead of grilling them right up and snarfing them down?)

If you haven't thought in advance to slice the sausages into 1-inch bits before freezing them, don't worry. Sausages are so full of fat that they slice easily, even when frozen.

1.

Press the button for	Set it for	Set the time for	If necessary, press
SAUTÉ	HIGH, MORE, or CUSTOM 400°F	10 minutes	START

2. Mix the sausage, marinara, broth, and seasoning blend in a **6- or 8-quart Instant Pot.** Cook, stirring occasionally, until many wisps of steam rise from the liquid. Turn off the SAUTÉ function; stir in the bell pepper strips and ziti. Lock the lid onto the pot.

3.

Set the machine for	Set the level for	The valve must be	And set the time for	If necessary, press
PRESSURE COOK	MAX	—	5 minutes with the KEEP WARM setting off	START
MEAT/STEW, PRESSURE COOK, or MANUAL	HIGH	Closed	6 minutes with the KEEP WARM setting off	START

4. Use the **quick-release method** to bring the pot's pressure back to normal. Unlatch the lid and open the cooker. Stir in the shredded cheese. Set the lid askew over the pot and set aside for 5 minutes to melt the cheese and let the pasta continue to absorb excess liquid. Serve by the big spoonful.

Beyond

- Use any frozen vegetables you like. But since pepper strips are classic, don't ditch them entirely, even if you want to add other frozen vegetables. Consider 8 ounces frozen bell pepper strips plus 8 ounces of another vegetable, even frozen chopped onion.

- Skip the purchased Italian seasoning and make your own blend: Combine 1 teaspoon dried oregano, ½ teaspoon dried rosemary, ½ teaspoon dried thyme, ½ teaspoon grated nutmeg, and ½ teaspoon fennel seeds.

- Garnish the servings with stemmed and minced fresh herbs, particularly parsley and oregano.

- And/or drizzle a little balsamic vinegar over each serving.

 Using a **-20°F CHEST FREEZER?** There is no difference in cooking times.

Creamy Sausage and Noodle Casserole

4–6 servings

2 cups chicken or vegetable broth

12 ounces <u>frozen</u> breakfast sausage patties (turkey, pork, beef, or vegetarian; gluten-free, if that is a concern)

1½ teaspoons stemmed and minced fresh sage leaves, or ½ teaspoon dried sage

1 teaspoon onion powder

½ teaspoon ground black pepper

12 ounces regular, no-yolk, or gluten-free dried egg noodles

One 12-ounce can regular or low-fat evaporated milk

1 cup regular or low-fat sour cream

Although this recipe uses frozen breakfast sausage patties, it's more of a savory, easy lunch or dinner than a breakfast dish. The patties come apart under pressure, spreading little bits of highly flavored meat throughout the sauce. You can use any sort of frozen sausage patty you like, but we recommend avoiding those that are "maple-flavored," which will turn the dish cloyingly sweet.

1. Mix the broth, sausage, sage, onion powder, and pepper in a **6- or 8-quart Instant Pot.** Lock the lid onto the cooker.

2.

Set the machine for	Set the level for	The valve must be	And set the time for	If necessary, press
PRESSURE COOK	MAX	—	1 minute with the KEEP WARM setting off	START
MEAT/STEW, PRESSURE COOK, or MANUAL	HIGH	Closed	1 minute with the KEEP WARM setting off	START

3. Use the **quick-release method** to bring the pot's pressure back to normal. Unlatch the lid and open the cooker. Use the edge of a large metal spoon or a metal spatula to break the sausage patties into very small bits. Stir in the noodles and evaporated milk until uniform. Lock the lid back onto the pot.

4.

Set the machine for	Set the level for	The valve must be	And set the time for	If necessary, press
PRESSURE COOK	MAX	—	3 minutes with the KEEP WARM setting off	START
MEAT/STEW, PRESSURE COOK, or MANUAL	HIGH	Closed	4 minutes with the KEEP WARM setting off	START

5. Use the **quick-release method** once again to bring the pot's pressure back to normal. Unlatch the lid and open the cooker. Wait for the bubbling to stop, then stir in the sour cream until uniform. Set the lid over the top of the pot and let sit for a couple of minutes to blend the flavors as the pasta continues to absorb some of the liquid.

Beyond

- For more oomph, add up to 1 tablespoon stemmed and minced fresh parsley leaves and/or ½ teaspoon fennel seeds and/or up to 2 teaspoons red pepper flakes with the sage.

 Using a **-20°F CHEST FREEZER?** There is no difference in cooking times.

Tortellini Primavera

4–6 servings

1 pound (4 to 5 cups) <u>frozen</u> mixed vegetables, preferably an "Italian" variety with bell peppers and peas in the mix

One 28-ounce can diced tomatoes packed in juice (3½ cups)

3 cups chicken or vegetable broth

1½ tablespoons dried Italian seasoning blend

Two 12-ounce boxes or bags <u>frozen</u> cheese tortellini

8 ounces (2 cups) shredded mozzarella or provolone cheese

Frozen tortellini make an easy meal in the Instant Pot. As with the Road Map: Ravioli (pages 48–49), the trick here is to make sure the liquid in the pot is hot (not simmering) before adding the tortellini. And the thicker sauce will ensure that the frozen, stuffed pasta doesn't quickly fall to the pot's bottom.

While primavera often has cream, it actually doesn't have to. We've left it out of the base recipe. See the *Beyond* section for adding some to the dish.

1.

Press the button for	Set it for	Set the time for	If necessary, press
SAUTÉ	HIGH, MORE, or CUSTOM 400°F	10 minutes	START

2. Stir the vegetables, tomatoes, broth, and Italian seasoning in a **6- or 8-quart Instant Pot.** Cook, stirring occasionally, until many wisps of steam rise from the liquid. Turn off the SAUTÉ function, stir in the frozen tortellini, and lock the lid onto the pot.

3.

Set the machine for	Set the level for	The valve must be	And set the time for	If necessary, press
PRESSURE COOK	MAX	—	2 minutes with the KEEP WARM setting off	START
SOUP/BROTH, PRESSURE COOK, or MANUAL	HIGH	Closed	3 minutes with the KEEP WARM setting off	START

4. Use the **quick-release method** to bring the pot's pressure back to normal. Unlatch the lid and open the cooker. Sprinkle the cheese evenly over the top of the casserole. Set the lid askew over the pot and let sit for 5 minutes to melt the cheese and let the pasta continue to absorb some of the liquid. Serve warm.

 Using a **-20°F CHEST FREEZER?** There is no difference in cooking times.

Beyond

- If you want to go beyond a bottled Italian seasoning blend, substitute 2 teaspoons dried rosemary, 2 teaspoons dried oregano, 1 teaspoon dried thyme, and ½ teaspoon dried sage for the blend.

- Or skip the dried seasoning and use up to 2 tablespoons purchased pesto instead.

- Add up to 1 tablespoon peeled and minced garlic with the vegetables. Or better, get three to five roasted garlic cloves from the supermarket's salad bar and add these with the vegetables.

- Stir ½ cup heavy or light cream into the dish before sprinkling with the cheese in step 4.

Easy Scallops Alfredo

4 servings

One 16-ounce jar alfredo sauce
(1¾ cups)

2½ cups chicken or vegetable
broth

½ teaspoon dried oregano

½ teaspoon garlic powder

½ teaspoon red pepper flakes

12 ounces regular, no-yolk, or
gluten-free dried egg noodles

1 pound <u>frozen</u> bay scallops

We developed this pasta casserole with frozen *bay* scallops (rather than
sea scallops) because bay scallops cook quickly and are readily available in
the freezer section of most large supermarkets. If you can't find them, use
frozen, raw, *small* peeled and deveined shrimp (about 50 per pound — not
the so-called "salad" shrimp, but small "standard" shrimp).

Some jarred alfredo sauces contain less than 16 ounces. If yours is
14½ or 15 ounces, add another 2 tablespoons broth in step 1.

1. Put 1½ cups of the alfredo sauce in a **6- or 8-quart Instant Pot.** Stir in
the broth, oregano, garlic powder, and red pepper flakes until smooth. Stir
in the noodles, then set the block of frozen scallops right on top. Lock the
lid onto the pot.

2.

Set the machine for	Set the level for	The valve must be	And set the time for	If necessary, press
PRESSURE COOK	MAX	—	3 minutes with the KEEP WARM setting off	START
MEAT/STEW, PRESSURE COOK, or MANUAL	HIGH	Closed	4 minutes with the KEEP WARM setting off	START

3. When the machine has finished cooking, turn it off and let its pressure **return to normal naturally** for 1 minute. Then use the **quick-release method** to get rid of any residual pressure in the pot.

4. Unlatch the lid and open the cooker. Stir in the remaining ¼ cup alfredo sauce. Set the lid askew over the pot and let sit for a couple of minutes so the noodles continue to absorb some of the liquid. Serve hot.

Beyond

- Add up to 1 cup frozen or fresh peas. Scatter them on top of the scallops in step 1 before locking on the lid.

- Garnish the servings with shredded Asiago cheese, or even a finely grated aged Asiago. Or just try finely grated Parmigiano-Reggiano.

- And/or garnish with stemmed and minced fresh parsley leaves.

- And/or garnish with lots of fresh black pepper.

 Using a **-20°F CHEST FREEZER?** There is no difference in cooking times.

3

Chicken and Turkey

Turning a frozen piece of chicken or an ice-solid block of ground turkey into a satisfying meal seems like kitchen wizardry. In fact, it's just a matter of controlling the overall liquid levels in the pot so the meat thaws and cooks before it dries out.

The one problem is the skin. With fresh chicken and turkey, you can pull it off and season the meat, or brown the skin before cooking it under pressure. You can't do either with a frozen bone-in breast. To solve this problem, we occasionally call for broiling chicken pieces for a minute or two after they come out of the pot to make them tastier. This step may be one too far for you. You can *always* omit it. For us, it's worth the hassle. But we don't have kids banging pots for dinner at 5:30 p.m.

Of course, these recipes are made for people who buy big bags of frozen chicken breasts or wings. But if you've bought fresh stuff and intend to store it in the freezer for a later use, do yourself a favor and remove the chicken, turkey, or even ground turkey from its packaging (discarding the "diaper" or gel pad inside). Seal the meat in a storage bag and freeze it separately. By planning ahead, you'll save yourself some hassle, because getting the "diaper" off frozen chicken is a pain in the neck. (But if you forgot to discard the diaper, we share a few tricks for getting it off on page 5.)

And one more thing: If your supermarket sells a bag of frozen chicken breasts, thighs, or wings that seems more like a big, solid chunk of ice, the contents of the bag have thawed (for whatever reason) and then refrozen into a mess. Our best advice is to find another supermarket. No convenience is worth shoddy storage practices.

Road Map: **Boneless Skinless Chicken Breasts**

Up to 6 servings

1½ cups liquid
Choose one or several to make the total volume from water, broth of any sort, wine of any sort, beer of any sort, or unsweetened apple cider.

Up to six 5- to 6-ounce frozen boneless skinless chicken breasts

Up to 1 tablespoon dried seasoning blend
Choose from Italian, Provençal, Cajun, Creole, taco seasoning, or another you prefer or create from dried spices.

Up to 1½ teaspoons table salt, optional (check to see if the seasoning blend includes salt)

Your dream for weeknight cooking might be simply getting a decent frozen chicken breast cooked and on a plate quickly. The Instant Pot is the best way we know to do this, period, no doubts. Better than the oven. Better than the stovetop. Better than any other way we've tried.

Pay careful attention to the size of the chicken breasts here: They are neither the tiny, 4-ounce ones nor the humongous, 10-ounce ones often found fresh in the meat case. The ones called for here are moderately sized (5 or 6 ounces) and often found in bags in the freezer case of supermarkets and big-box retailers.

If you've used any liquid besides plain water (even if you've used a combination of water and another liquid), consider turning the resulting stock in the pot into a sauce: Remove the rack from the pot, set the SAUTÉ setting on HIGH for 15 minutes, and boil the liquid until it is a thick glaze, stirring occasionally. Whisk in up to 3 tablespoons butter, then turn off the SAUTÉ function and remove the (hot!) insert from the pot to stop the cooking (so the butter doesn't fall out of suspension and burn). Drizzle the sauce over the chicken and serve.

1. Pour the liquid into a **6-quart Instant Pot.** Set the pot's rack (with the handles up) or a large, open vegetable steamer inside the pot. Set the chicken breasts on the rack or in the steamer, stacking them in a crisscross manner (so there's room for steam to circulate among them), sort of like horizontal planks put this way and that. Sprinkle each breast with ½ teaspoon dried seasoning blend and ¼ teaspoon salt (if using). Lock the lid onto the pot.

2.

Set the machine for	Set the level for	The valve must be	And set the time for	If necessary, press
PRESSURE COOK	MAX	—	12 minutes with the KEEP WARM setting off	START
POULTRY, PRESSURE COOK, or MANUAL	HIGH	Closed	15 minutes with the KEEP WARM setting off	START

3. Use the **quick-release method** to bring the pot's pressure back to normal. Unlatch the lid and open the cooker. Use kitchen tongs to transfer the chicken breasts to a serving platter. Serve hot — or cover and store in the fridge for up to 3 days.

❄ Using a **-20°F CHEST FREEZER?** There is no difference in cooking times.

Beyond

- For an **8-quart Instant Pot,** you must use 2 cups liquid.

- The meat has not been browned. If you'd like a "browned" look (without any actual browning), lightly dust each breast with mild paprika before adding the dried seasoning blend.

- Good liquid/spice pairings include dry white wine and a Provençal blend of dried herbs (sometimes called "herbes de Provence"); amber beer and taco seasoning blend; and unsweetened apple cider and poultry seasoning blend.

- Make your own dried seasoning blend out of a mix of dried parsley, thyme, tarragon, and/or oregano, varying the amounts based on your taste. Or try a mix of equal parts dried parsley, thyme, and dill.

- Make the warm breasts into a meal by setting them over a chopped salad of mixed greens plus crunchy vegetables like bell peppers, broccoli florets, and/or celery. (You can find most of these things pre-prepped in the supermarket's produce section — and sometimes in smaller quantities in the salad bar.) Dress the salad with olive oil, balsamic vinegar, salt, pepper, and a little dried oregano.

Road Map: **Bone-In Chicken Breasts**

Up to 6 servings

1 cup liquid

Choose from water, broth of any sort, wine of any sort, beer of any sort, unsweetened apple cider, or a combination of any of these.

Up to six 12- to 14-ounce frozen bone-in skin-on chicken breasts

Up to 2 tablespoons dried seasoning blend

Choose from Provençal, Cajun, poultry, taco, Italian, or another blend you prefer or create.

Up to 1½ teaspoons table salt, optional (check to see if the seasoning blend includes salt)

Unlike boneless breasts, bone-in chicken breasts are thicker and thus benefit from being set down in the liquid in the pot (rather than up on a rack or in a steamer). You'll use less liquid here than with our technique for boneless skinless breasts because these breasts will thaw and release water and other liquid into the pot as they cook.

Because of the way the bones add a distinct depth of flavor to the meat, bone-in chicken breasts are a great choice if you want to debone and chop the meat for chicken salad and pasta salad, or to slice the meat for sandwiches.

Be forewarned: You must check the internal temperature of the meat with an instant-read meat thermometer. Bone-in breasts have varying thicknesses — and varying amounts of internal moisture depending on whether they've been injected with a brining solution. While our timing worked several times in testing, there are safety concerns with eating undercooked poultry. Better safe than sorry. See step 3 for more details on checking the meat's internal temperature.

Finally, to get the skin crisp, transfer the cooked breasts skin side up onto a lipped baking sheet. Set the oven rack about 6 inches from the broiler, heat the broiler, then brown the breasts under it for 1–2 minutes.

1. Pour the liquid into a **6-quart Instant Pot.** Position the bone-in chicken breasts in the liquid in a crisscross pattern (rather than stacking them on top of each other) so that steam can circulate among them. Sprinkle the top of each with 1 teaspoon dried seasoning blend and ¼ teaspoon salt (if using). Lock the lid onto the pot.

2.

Set the machine for	Set the level for	The valve must be	And set the time for	If necessary, press
PRESSURE COOK	MAX	—	35 minutes with the KEEP WARM setting off	START
POULTRY, PRESSURE COOK, or MANUAL	HIGH	Closed	40 minutes with the KEEP WARM setting off	START

3. Use the **quick-release method** to bring the pot's pressure back to normal. Unlatch the lid and open the cooker. Insert an instant-read meat thermometer into the center of a couple of the breasts, without touching bone, to make sure their internal temperature is 165°F. The meat can be a little pink at the bone and still perfectly safe to eat, *so long as* its internal temperature is correct. If the internal temperature is below 165°F (or if you're worried about the color), lock the lid back onto the pot and give the breasts 3 extra minutes at MAX, or 4 minutes at HIGH. Again, use the **quick-release method** to bring the pot's pressure back to normal.

4. Use kitchen tongs to transfer the breasts to serving plates or a serving platter to serve. Or cool them at room temperature for 10 minutes or so, then store in a sealed container in the fridge for up to 3 days.

 Using a **−20°F CHEST FREEZER?** Cook under pressure in step 2 for 40 minutes on the MAX setting, or for 45 minutes on the HIGH setting, followed by a **quick release.**

Beyond

- For an **8-quart Instant Pot,** you must use 1½ cups liquid. You can also fit up to eight 12- to 14-ounce bone-in chicken breasts in the larger pot. There is no change in the cooking timing under pressure (although the pot will take longer to come to pressure).

- If you've used water and/or broth, the resulting liquid in the pot is an astounding chicken stock. Don't throw it out! Save it in a sealed container in the fridge for up to 2 days or in the freezer for up to 3 months. Use it in place of chicken broth in any recipe.

- Consider making the liquid in the pot a 50-50 split of broth and the brine from a jar of pickles, pepperoncini, or pickled jalapeño rings. In this case, omit the salt. (And the remaining liquid in the pot won't be fit to be used as stock.)

Road Map: **Roast Chicken**
4–6 servings

1½ cups liquid

Choose from water, chicken broth, white wine of any sort, a light-colored beer of any sort, unsweetened apple cider, or a combination of two or even three of these liquids.

One 3½- to 4½-pound <u>frozen</u> whole chicken (see page 5 for tips on getting the wrapper off the chicken)

Nonstick spray of any flavor (but *not* baking spray)

1 tablespoon dried seasoning blend

Choose from Italian, Cajun, poultry, za'atar, or your preferred (or created) blend.

1 teaspoon table salt, optional (check to see if the seasoning blend includes salt)

Okay, "roast" is a misnomer. But you can prepare a whole frozen chicken in the pot, sort of like a roast chicken but with much less fuss (and cleanup). This recipe requires a two-step process so you can stop the cooking to remove the giblets and neck from the bird. We've seen internet videos in which people cook a frozen chicken, giblets and all, in one step. But then the liver and other innards thaw and overcook, giving the meat a funky flavor. Blech.

Note that a 4½-pound frozen chicken will just about fill a 6-quart pot. It will sit up above the MAX FILL line. But the liquid won't — so there are no worries.

To maneuver the whole chicken in the pot, it's best to put it on the pot's rack (with the handles up). Even then, the liquid may come up over the handles. You can't stick your fingers in the hot liquids. You'll have to use tongs to pull the rack up a bit.

1. Pour the liquid into a **6- or 8-quart Instant Pot.** Set the pot's rack (with the handles up) or a large, open vegetable steamer inside the pot.

2. Spray the frozen chicken breast and sides with nonstick spray, then coat with the seasoning mix and salt (if using). Set the chicken breast-side up on the rack (and thus between its handles) or in the steamer. Lock the lid onto the pot.

3.

Set the machine for	Set the level for	The valve must be	And set the time for	If necessary, press
PRESSURE COOK	MAX	—	40 minutes with the KEEP WARM setting off	START
POULTRY, PRESSURE COOK, or MANUAL	HIGH	Closed	45 minutes with the KEEP WARM setting off	START

4. Use the **quick-release method** to bring the pot's pressure back to normal. Unlatch the lid and open the cooker. Use silicone cooking mitts or kitchen tongs and thick hot pads to lift the rack with the chicken out of the cooker; set it all in a clean sink. (If you can't put the cooker next to the sink, you'll need to transfer the chicken on its rack to a very large bowl.)

5. Use kitchen tongs to grasp and pull out the chicken neck and the bag of giblets from either the large hole on one side of the chicken or perhaps from each of the holes on either side of the chicken. Make sure the bird is breast-side up on the rack and return it to the pot. Lock the lid back onto the cooker.

6.

Set the machine for	Set the level for	The valve must be	And set the time for	If necessary, press
PRESSURE COOK	MAX	—	15 minutes with the KEEP WARM setting off	START
POULTRY, PRESSURE COOK, or MANUAL	HIGH	Closed	20 minutes with the KEEP WARM setting off	START

7. When the machine has finished cooking, turn it off and let its pressure **return to normal naturally,** about 25 minutes. Unlatch the lid and open the cooker. Insert an instant-read meat thermometer into the center of the thickest part of one thigh without touching bone. The temperature should read 165°F. If not, lock the lid back onto the pot and give it another 5 minutes at MAX or 7 minutes at HIGH followed by a **quick release.**

8. Cool the chicken in the cooker for a couple of minutes, then set a large cutting board next to the cooker and use silicone cooking mitts or thick hot pads to transfer the chicken on its rack to the cutting board. Remove the rack, cool a couple more minutes, then carve or slice the chicken as desired.

Beyond

- For an **8-quart Instant Pot,** you *can* use a frozen chicken up to 5½ pounds. But then you *must* cook the chicken for 55 minutes at MAX or 1 hour on HIGH in step 3.

- The chicken has not been browned. Once cooked, you can cut it into large pieces (the breasts, the thighs-and-leg quarters), then lay these skin-side down on a lipped baking sheet. Position the oven rack 6 inches from the broiler, heat the broiler, and broil the chicken pieces, turning once, until browned, 2–3 minutes. (If you try to brown the whole chicken at once, one side will burn while another won't even change color.)

- If you've used water, broth, or a combination of the two, you'll end up with an incredible chicken stock. Either bring it to a boil on the SAUTÉ setting at HIGH, MORE, or CUSTOM 400°F for 10 minutes or so to concentrate it a bit, or just use it as it is from the pot for a slightly thinner, weaker stock. Either way, freeze it in covered, 1-cup containers to add a fantastic chicken flavor to any recipe that calls for chicken broth.

Using a **-20°F CHEST FREEZER?** Cook under pressure in step 3 for 50 minutes on MAX, or for 55 minutes on the HIGH setting.

Road Map: **Chicken Stew**

4 servings

1 cup chicken or vegetable broth

½ cup frozen chopped onion; or 1 small yellow or white onion, peeled and chopped

Up to 3 sprigs of a single fresh herb

Choose from fresh basil, oregano, parsley, rosemary, sage, tarragon, or thyme.

Up to 2 teaspoons peeled and minced garlic, optional

½ teaspoon table salt

½ teaspoon ground black pepper

2 pounds frozen boneless skinless chicken thighs

10 ounces (2 cups) frozen unseasoned hash brown cubes

12 ounces (3 cups) frozen unseasoned chopped vegetables of any sort

Choose one or two vegetables (like bell pepper strips and broccoli florets or corn and cauliflower florets) or use a purchased blend of vegetables.

4 tablespoons (½ stick) butter, optional

2 tablespoons all-purpose flour, optional

Here's a terrific way to make a fast, comforting stew. It seems everyone wants to use boneless skinless chicken breasts for a recipe like this, but that white meat dries out too quickly, given the way it has to thaw and cook with this technique. Boneless skinless thighs are better: tastier, juicier, less apt to turn into shards.

Remember that some herbs are more powerful than others. Rosemary, tarragon—these are big flavors, so consider using only one sprig. Or use a couple of different types of herbs—say, one rosemary sprig and two oregano sprigs.

Steps 6 through 8 (to thicken the stew) are actually optional. The stew will be much thinner without those steps, too much so for our taste but perhaps a fine alternative if you're in a rush.

1. Mix the broth, onion, herbs, garlic (if using), salt, and pepper in a **6-quart Instant Pot.** Set the pot's rack (with the handles up) or a large, open vegetable steamer inside the pot. Place the block or chunks of frozen thighs on the rack or in the steamer. (You may have to set a big, flat block of frozen thighs on a cutting board and use an ice pick, a cleaver, an oyster shucker, or even a very well-cleaned screwdriver to pry it into two or three parts that will fit in the cooker.) Lock the lid onto the pot.

2.

Set the machine for	Set the level for	The valve must be	And set the time for	If necessary, press
PRESSURE COOK	MAX	—	12 minutes with the KEEP WARM setting off	START
POULTRY, PRESSURE COOK, or MANUAL	HIGH	Closed	15 minutes with the KEEP WARM setting off	START

3. Use the **quick-release method** to bring the pot's pressure back to normal. Unlatch the lid and open the cooker. Use silicone cooking mitts or thick hot pads to lift up and remove the rack or steamer, letting the thighs fall into the liquid below. Stir in the hash brown cubes and vegetables. Lock the lid back onto the pot.

4.

Set the machine for	Set the level for	The valve must be	And set the time for	If necessary, press
PRESSURE COOK	MAX	——	2 minutes with the KEEP WARM setting off	START
POULTRY, PRESSURE COOK, or MANUAL	HIGH	Closed	3 minutes with the KEEP WARM setting off	START

5. Again, use the **quick-release method** to bring the pot's pressure back to normal. Unlatch the lid and open the cooker. Fish out and discard the herb sprigs. If desired, cut each chicken thigh into two or three pieces right in the pot. (Kitchen shears work best.)

6. If thickening the stew, melt the butter in a small microwave-safe bowl in a microwave on high in 10-second bursts, stopping after each, until melted (even if partway through one of the bursts). Use a fork or a small whisk to whisk the flour into the butter until smooth.

7.

Press the button for	Set it for	Set the time for	If necessary, press
SAUTÉ	HIGH, MORE, or CUSTOM 400°F	10 minutes	START

8. Bring the stew to a full simmer, then stir the butter mixture into the stew by dribs and drabs. Continue cooking, stirring constantly, until thickened, about 1 minute. Turn off the SAUTÉ setting and set the pot aside for a couple of minutes for the stew to set up. Serve hot in big bowls.

Beyond

- For an **8-quart Instant Pot,** you must add ½ cup additional broth. Or add ½ cup additional broth and increase boneless skinless chicken thighs to 3 pounds; or just increase all the ingredients by 50 percent.

- For a sweeter stew, use a 50-50 combo of broth and a dry white wine, or a 75-25 combo of broth and unsweetened apple cider.

- If desired, stir up to ½ cup heavy or light cream (but not fat-free) into the stew with the butter paste in step 8.

Using a **–20°F CHEST FREEZER?** There is no difference in cooking times.

Chicken Fajitas

6 servings

1 large onion, peeled, halved,
    and sliced into thin
    half-moons

¾ cup chicken broth

One 12-ounce package fajita
    seasoning (a gluten-free
    version, if that's a concern)

2 tablespoons pickled jalapeño
    rings with some of the
    pickling juice

2 pounds <u>frozen</u> chicken
    tenders

1 pound (4 cups) <u>frozen</u> bell
    pepper strips

Fajitas are so easy when you start with frozen chicken tenders! You may need to cut the tenders into smaller bits before serving them, depending on how stuffed you like the tortillas. We prefer them filled to the brim with whole tenders in the mix. You may want to take more, um, delicate bites. The best way to cut them to bits is to use kitchen shears after cooking.

The pickling brine from the jalapeño rings adds salt and a little sour kick to the dish. The amount you use is not crucial (there's already enough liquid in the pot). Just stick a tablespoon into the jar and pull out some of the rings with their brine. A little more or less won't change the overall character of the dish.

Unfortunately, because of the way the timing works in this recipe, you can't use fresh bell pepper strips. They get too soggy with the longer cooking time that the chicken tenders require.

1. Place the onion slices in a **6-quart Instant Pot.** Add the broth, half the seasoning blend, and all the pickled jalapeño rings with their juice and stir well. Set the pot's rack (with its handles up) or a large, open vegetable steamer in this mixture.

2. Set half the chicken tenders on the rack. Sprinkle them with half the remaining seasoning blend (that is, a quarter of the original volume). Top with the remaining chicken tenders and sprinkle with the remaining seasoning blend. Top everything with the bell pepper strips. Do not stir or toss. Lock the lid onto the pot.

3.

Set the machine for	Set the level for	The valve must be	And set the time for	If necessary, press
PRESSURE COOK	MAX	—	12 minutes with the KEEP WARM setting off	START
POULTRY, PRESSURE COOK, or MANUAL	HIGH	Closed	15 minutes with the KEEP WARM setting off	START

4. Use the **quick-release method** to bring the pot's pressure back to normal. Unlatch the lid and open the cooker. Use kitchen tongs, silicone cooking mitts, or thick hot pads to remove the rack or steamer from the pot, letting the chicken fall into the sauce below. Stir well.

5.

Press the button for	Set it for	Set the time for	If necessary, press
SAUTÉ	HIGH, MORE, or CUSTOM 400°F	15 minutes	START

6. As the sauce comes to a simmer, use a slotted spoon to transfer the chicken tenders and the vegetables to a serving platter. Boil the sauce, stirring often, until reduced to a glaze, about 10 minutes. Turn off the SAUTÉ function and pour the sauce over the chicken and vegetables before serving.

 Using a **–20°F CHEST FREEZER?** There is no difference in cooking times.

Beyond

- For an **8-quart Instant Pot,** you must either use 1¼ cups broth or increase all the ingredients by 50 percent. (The sauce will take up to 5 minutes longer to reduce in step 6.)

- This recipe delivers only the chicken and vegetables for fajitas. You'll also need warmed flour or corn tortillas; peeled, pitted, and thinly sliced avocados; shredded Monterey Jack, Cheddar, or Swiss cheese (or even a purchased Tex-Mex blend); minced scallions; sour cream; and/or stemmed, minced fresh cilantro leaves.

- If you want to make your own seasoning blend, skip the packet and mix the following in a small bowl: 1 tablespoon chili powder, 1 tablespoon mild smoked paprika, 1 tablespoon ground cumin, 1 tablespoon dried oregano, 2 teaspoons dark brown sugar, and 1 teaspoon table salt.

Chicken Teriyaki

4–6 servings

¾ cup chicken broth

½ cup regular or reduced-sodium soy sauce or tamari

½ cup **frozen** chopped onion; or 1 small yellow or white onion, peeled and chopped

3 tablespoons light brown sugar

2 tablespoons peeled and minced fresh ginger

1 tablespoon peeled and minced garlic

3 pounds **frozen** boneless skinless chicken thighs

Why use bottled teriyaki sauce when it's so easy to make your own with all the "chicken goodness" in the pot from the meat thawing and cooking? Teriyaki is usually grilled, of course. To make a successful version of teriyaki in the pot, it's best to cook the chicken in the aromatic sauce, then boil that sauce down to a thick glaze to use as a coating for the meat. Think of its final viscosity as about like duck sauce or Thai sweet chili sauce. Stir a lot as it cooks down because the sugars can start to burn.

1. Mix the broth, soy sauce or tamari, onion, brown sugar, ginger, and garlic in a **6-quart** Instant Pot. Add the block or hunks of frozen chicken, stir well, and lock the lid onto the pot.

2.

Set the machine for	Set the level for	The valve must be	And set the time for	If necessary, press
PRESSURE COOK	MAX	—	17 minutes with the KEEP WARM setting off	START
POULTRY, PRESSURE COOK, or MANUAL	HIGH	Closed	20 minutes with the KEEP WARM setting off	START

3. When the machine has finished cooking, turn it off and let its pressure **return to normal naturally,** about 25 minutes. Unlatch the lid and open the cooker. Use tongs or a slotted spoon to transfer the chicken thighs to a bowl.

4.

Press the button for	Set it for	Set the time for	If necessary, press
SAUTÉ	HIGH, MORE, or CUSTOM 400°F	15 minutes	START

5. Bring the sauce in the pot to a boil, stirring often. Continue boiling, stirring more and more frequently until almost constantly, until the sauce is a thick glaze, about 7 minutes. Turn off the SAUTÉ function. Return the chicken thighs and any juices to the cooker. Stir until the chicken is coated in the glaze. Transfer the pieces to a serving platter or plates.

 Using a **-20°F CHEST FREEZER?** There is no difference in cooking times.

Beyond

- For an **8-quart Instant Pot,** you must increase all the ingredients by 50 percent.

- Garnish the chicken with minced scallions and/or sesame seeds.

- Or drizzle with toasted sesame oil.

- Serve the chicken teriyaki over sticky, cooked, *short*-grain white rice (such as sushi rice) or cooked and drained millet.

Chicken, Rice, and Mushroom Casserole

4 servings

4 tablespoons (½ stick) unsalted butter

½ cup frozen chopped onion; or 1 small yellow or white onion, peeled and chopped

4 ounces (1 cup) sliced white or brown mushrooms

¾ cup raw white basmati rice (see page 9)

1⅓ cups chicken broth

Four frozen 5- to 6-ounce boneless skinless chicken breasts

1 tablespoon dried Italian seasoning blend

½ teaspoon table salt, optional (check to see if the seasoning blend includes salt)

This recipe is a version of the American standard: a buttery casserole for a weeknight indulgence. While the chicken steams over rice, some of the meat's natural juices drip into the rice, making it tastier.

The *only* way to make this dish work without activating the pot's burn notice is *to use a vegetable steamer, not the pot's rack (or trivet)*. The steamer should have legs about 2 inches tall for the frozen chicken to stand out of the liquid enough to keep the liquid from cooling down (and therefore letting some of the rice grains stick to the pot's bottom before the liquid can come to a fast boil and the pot can come to pressure). All this malarkey may seem like unwarranted fussiness, but it's the only way to guarantee success.

And note the size of those boneless skinless chicken breasts: They are neither giant nor tiny. Only 5- to 6-ounce cuts will cook in the time it takes the rice to get tender.

1.

Press the button for	Set it for	Set the time for	If necessary, press
SAUTÉ	MEDIUM, NORMAL, or CUSTOM 400°F	5 minutes	START

2. Melt 2 tablespoons butter in a **6-quart Instant Pot.** Add the onion and mushrooms; cook, stirring often, until the mushrooms give off their liquid, 3–4 minutes.

3. Stir in the rice until the grains are coated in the liquid, then stir in the broth. Turn off the SAUTÉ function and set a large, open vegetable steamer inside over the rice mixture.

4. Set the frozen chicken breasts in the steamer, overlapping them like shingles without stacking them on top of each other. Sprinkle them with the seasoning blend and salt (if using), then set the remaining 2 tablespoons of butter on top of them. Lock the lid onto the pot.

5.

Set the machine for	Set the level for	The valve must be	And set the time for	If necessary, press
PRESSURE COOK	MAX	—	10 minutes with the KEEP WARM setting off	START
POULTRY, PRESSURE COOK, or MANUAL	HIGH	Closed	12 minutes with the KEEP WARM setting off	START

6. Use the **quick-release method** to bring the pot's pressure back to normal. Unlatch the lid and open the cooker. Use tongs to transfer the chicken breasts to a serving platter or serving plates. Remove the steamer. Serve the rice alongside the breasts.

Beyond

• For an **8-quart Instant Pot,** you must increase all the ingredients by 50 percent.

• For a fresher flavor, omit the dried Italian seasoning blend and sprinkle the breasts with 1 tablespoon stemmed and minced fresh oregano leaves, 1 tablespoon stemmed and minced fresh parsley leaves, and 1 teaspoon stemmed and minced fresh rosemary leaves. Also add ½ teaspoon table salt with the rice.

❄ Using a **-20°F CHEST FREEZER?** There is no difference in cooking times.

Quick Arroz con Pollo

6 servings

One 28-ounce can whole
   tomatoes packed in juice
   (3½ cups)

1 cup chicken broth

2 teaspoons stemmed and
   minced fresh oregano leaves,
   or 1 teaspoon dried oregano

2 teaspoons stemmed fresh
   thyme leaves, or 1 teaspoon
   dried thyme

1 teaspoon mild smoked
   paprika

½ teaspoon table salt

Up to ½ teaspoon red pepper
   flakes

2 pounds frozen boneless
   skinless chicken thighs

1¾ cups raw white basmati rice
   (see page 9)

1 cup frozen peas or shelled
   fresh peas

While not necessarily an easy recipe, this one is certainly faster than the oven standard! Consider ours a well-stocked pilaf with the flavors of the classic Spanish rice dish.

If you've got leftovers, make chicken-and-rice patties: Cut the chicken thighs into small bits, then mix them into the rice and vegetables. Store in a covered container in the fridge for up to 2 days. Mix a large egg into this mixture and form into approximately ½-inch-thick patties. Fry in some olive oil in a nonstick skillet over medium heat, gently turning once, until golden brown, about 6 minutes.

1. Drain the liquid from the canned tomatoes into a **6- or 8-quart Instant Pot** (reserving the whole tomatoes for step 4). Stir in the broth, oregano, thyme, smoked paprika, salt, and red pepper flakes. Set the pot's rack (with the handles up) or a large, open vegetable steamer in the broth mixture. Place the blob of frozen chicken thighs on the rack or in the steamer. You can try to break the chicken up into a few pieces (see page 80, step 1, for an idea of how to do that) or slant the clump on its side against the pot's insert. Lock the lid onto the pot.

2.

Set the machine for	Set the level for	The valve must be	And set the time for	If necessary, press
PRESSURE COOK	MAX	——	8 minutes with the KEEP WARM setting off	START
POULTRY, PRESSURE COOK, or MANUAL	HIGH	Closed	10 minutes with the KEEP WARM setting off	START

3. Use the **quick-release method** to bring the pot's pressure back to normal. Unlatch the lid and open the cooker. Use kitchen tongs, silicone cooking mitts, or thick hot pads to remove the rack or steamer from the pot, letting the thighs fall into the liquid below. Separate any thighs stuck together into individual pieces.

4. Use clean hands to crush the reserved whole canned tomatoes into the cooker. Stir in the rice and peas. Lock the lid back onto the pot.

5.

Set the machine for	Set the level for	The valve must be	And set the time for	If necessary, press
PRESSURE COOK	MAX	—	10 minutes with the KEEP WARM setting off	START
MEAT/STEW, PRESSURE COOK, or MANUAL	HIGH	Closed	12 minutes with the KEEP WARM setting off	START

6. Again, use the **quick-release method** to bring the pot's pressure back to normal — but this time, do not open the pot. *Set it aside with the lid on but the pressure valve open for 10 minutes.* Unlatch the lid and open the cooker. Stir the contents of the pot until everything's uniform. Serve hot.

Beyond

- For a more authentic dish, add ⅛ teaspoon saffron threads with the other spices.

- For more heft, add up to 1 cup frozen pearl onions with the broth in step 1.

 Using a **-20°F CHEST FREEZER?** There is no difference in cooking times.

Buffalo Chicken Wings

4–6 servings

½ cup red hot sauce, preferably Texas Pete or Frank's RedHot

¼ cup chicken broth

4 tablespoons (½ stick) butter, cut into three or four pieces

2 tablespoons dried Cajun seasoning blend (a gluten-free version, if that's a concern)

3 pounds not-breaded frozen chicken wings, preferably individually frozen wings (sometimes called "ice glazed")

½ cup regular or low-fat mayonnaise

½ cup regular or low-fat sour cream

2 ounces (½ cup) crumbled blue cheese

½ teaspoon onion powder

½ teaspoon ground black pepper

Frozen wings are so easy in the cooker! And so delicious. The wings thaw quickly and cook in no time. Although we assume you'll use both the wingette and the drumette portion of the wing, you can use just one or the other at your preference.

At the supermarket, look for individually frozen chicken wings. If you buy fresh wings on sale and want to freeze them, take the wings out of their packaging and freeze them in a fairly condensed hunk in a plastic bag for up to 3 months. In that case, you'll need to set the hunk on the cooker's rack, slanting up to the pot's insert, and cook on MAX for 18 minutes or on HIGH for 22 minutes, followed by a **quick release.** You'll also need to break the wings apart when you open the pot. If they're still not cooked through (because of the density of the mass), cook them for another 3 minutes on either MAX or HIGH followed by a **quick release.**

1. Stir the hot sauce, broth, butter, and seasoning blend in a **6-quart Instant Pot.** Set the wings in the sauce and toss well. Lock the lid onto the pot.

2.

Set the machine for	Set the level for	The valve must be	And set the time for	If necessary, press
PRESSURE COOK	MAX	—	12 minutes with the KEEP WARM setting off	START
POULTRY, PRESSURE COOK, or MANUAL	HIGH	Closed	15 minutes with the KEEP WARM setting off	START

3. Use the **quick-release method** to bring the pot's pressure back to normal. Unlatch the lid and open the cooker. Use tongs to transfer the wings to a large serving platter.

4. Whisk the mayonnaise, sour cream, blue cheese, onion powder, and pepper in a small bowl until creamy. Serve alongside the hot wings as a dip (perhaps with some of the boiled-down liquid from the machine for a second dip).

 Using a **-20°F CHEST FREEZER?** There is no difference in cooking times.

Beyond

- For an **8-quart Instant Pot,** you must increase all the ingredients by 50 percent.

- To make these wings crisp (and thus take them over the top): In step 3, use tongs to transfer them from the cooker to a large, lipped baking sheet. Position the oven rack about 4 inches from the broiler and heat the broiler. Broil the wings until crunchy, basting several times with the pot's juices and turning once, 2–3 minutes.

- Buffalo wings need celery and carrot sticks!

- Although this blue cheese dip is traditional, we'll confess we've come to like the wings with ranch dressing that's been mixed with minced pickled jalapeño rings and minced chives.

Chinese-Style Chicken Wings

4–6 servings

½ cup chicken broth

¼ cup regular or reduced-sodium soy sauce or tamari

2 tablespoons toasted sesame oil

2 tablespoons unseasoned rice vinegar (see headnote); or 1½ tablespoons apple cider vinegar

2 tablespoons light brown sugar

1 tablespoon peeled and minced fresh ginger

½ teaspoon five-spice powder

3 pounds not-breaded frozen chicken wings, preferably individually frozen wings (sometimes called "ice glazed")

This recipe makes the best wings for Game Day! They're sweet, moist, and irresistible. The recipe does, however, include a couple of ingredients that are less common than the others you'll find in this book. Here they are:

1. Rice vinegar is a low-acid vinegar made from fermented glutinous rice. It's available "unseasoned" (in other words, without sugar or a sweetener of some sort) and "seasoned" (with a sweetener). Usually, the "unsweetened" variety is not labeled as "unseasoned," but the "sweetened" one is labeled as "seasoned." Confusing? A bit. Check the ingredients listed on the labels to be sure there's no sweetening in the mix.

2. Five-spice powder is a blend of Chinese spices, including ground star anise, cloves, cinnamon, and fennel seeds. Better brands have ground Sichuan peppercorns in the mix. In truth, you could omit it in this recipe, but the final dish will be less aromatic. Consider adding ¼ teaspoon ground cinnamon in its place.

See the headnote to the other wing recipe (page 90) for how to deal with a block of frozen chicken wings, rather than ones that have been individually frozen.

1. Mix the broth, soy sauce or tamari, sesame oil, vinegar, brown sugar, ginger, and five-spice powder in a **6-quart Instant Pot.** Add the wings and toss to coat (as well as you can). Lock the lid onto the pot.

2.

Set the machine for	Set the level for	The valve must be	And set the time for	If necessary, press
PRESSURE COOK	MAX	—	12 minutes with the KEEP WARM setting off	START
POULTRY, PRESSURE COOK, or MANUAL	HIGH	Closed	15 minutes with the KEEP WARM setting off	START

3. Use the **quick-release method** to bring the pot's pressure back to normal. Unlatch the lid and open the cooker. Use tongs to transfer the wings to a serving platter. Serve hot.

Beyond

- For an **8-quart Instant Pot,** you must increase all the ingredients by 50 percent.

- To make these wings even better, in step 3 use tongs to transfer the wings from the cooker to a large, lipped baking sheet. Boil the liquid in the pot to a glaze by setting the SAUTÉ setting on HIGH and stirring occasionally, 7 minutes. Set the oven rack about 4 inches from the broiler and heat the broiler. Broil the wings, turning once, until crisp, about 3 minutes, brushing this glaze over the wings as they broil.

❄️ Using a **-20°F CHEST FREEZER?** There is no difference in cooking times.

Game Hens with Lemon Butter Sauce

2–4 servings

¾ cup water

2 tablespoons lemon juice

2 tablespoons butter

Two <u>frozen</u> 1- to 1½-pound game hens

1½ teaspoons lemon pepper seasoning

1 teaspoon table salt, optional (check to see if the lemon pepper blend includes salt)

Game hens often come frozen in packages of two. Now there's no reason to thaw them! No, they won't get browned and crisp. But a quick pass under the broiler renders them perfect in step 7.

The number of servings here is a somewhat wide range (two to four), depending on 1) appetites and 2) what other sides you have on the table.

1. Mix the water, lemon juice, and butter in a **6-quart Instant Pot.** Set the frozen game hens in the pot side by side (or as much as possible). Sprinkle the lemon-pepper seasoning and salt (if using) over the birds. Lock the lid onto the pot.

2.

Set the machine for	Set the level for	The valve must be	And set the time for	If necessary, press
PRESSURE COOK	MAX	—	30 minutes with the KEEP WARM setting off	START
POULTRY, PRESSURE COOK, or MANUAL	HIGH	Closed	40 minutes with the KEEP WARM setting off	START

3. When the machine has finished cooking, turn it off and let its pressure **return to normal naturally,** about 25 minutes.

4. Unlatch the lid and open the cooker. Use tongs to transfer the game hens to a cutting board. Cut them in half lengthwise (that is, on one side of the backbone and the breast bone). Set them skin-side up on a large, lipped baking sheet.

5.

Press the button for	Set it for	Set the time for	If necessary, press
SAUTÉ	HIGH, MORE, or CUSTOM 400°F	15 minutes	START

6. Bring the liquid in the cooker to a full boil. Boil, stirring often, until reduced to a thick glaze, about 7 minutes. Turn off the SAUTÉ function and remove the (hot!) insert from the pot to stop the cooking.

7. Position the oven rack about 6 inches from the broiler and heat the broiler. Broil the hens until crisp and brown, about 2 minutes. Transfer to a serving platter and mop with the glaze from the pot.

Beyond

- For an **8-quart Instant Pot,** you must increase the water to 1¼ cups and the lemon juice to 3 tablespoons. The sauce in the pot will take at least 10 minutes to boil down to a glaze in step 6.

- Change the flavor profile by using a different acid for the lemon juice (balsamic vinegar, red wine vinegar, unseasoned rice vinegar, or even lime juice) and a different seasoning blend (barbecue rub, Italian seasoning blend, powdered adobo mix, or jerk seasoning blend).

❄ Using a **-20°F CHEST FREEZER?** There is no difference in cooking times.

Turkey Tacos

6–8 servings

One 16-ounce jar chunky-style mild or hot red salsa (about 2 cups)

½ cup chicken broth

One 4½-ounce can chopped mild or hot green chiles (½ cup)

½ cup frozen chopped onion; or 1 small yellow or white onion, peeled and chopped

2 teaspoons standard chili powder

2 teaspoons ground cumin

½ teaspoon ground cinnamon

¼ teaspoon table salt, optional (check the salt content of the salsa)

Two 1-pound packages frozen ground turkey

2 tablespoons yellow cornmeal

Soft flour or corn tortillas or taco shells, for serving

Shredded lettuce, for serving

Shredded cheese, for serving

We designed this recipe to make *a lot* of taco filling because 1) that filling is tasty enough for crowds, and 2) it freezes well for quick, microwave meals in the weeks or months ahead.

You'll need two 1-pound packages of ground turkey (rather than one 2-pound package). The blocks of frozen meat need to stand against each other in the cooker. Otherwise, they have a tendency to scorch — or one gets done while the other stays partially frozen.

Frozen ground turkey can be difficult to break apart. After cooking, it stays in long, thin strands, about the way it comes out of the grinder. You'll need to break these into smaller bits for a good taco filling.

1. Stir the salsa, broth, chiles, onion, chili powder, cumin, cinnamon, and salt (if using) in a **6-quart Instant Pot.** Set the two blocks of frozen turkey in the pot so that they look like an A-frame or a lean-to, sticking up out of the liquid and balancing against each other along their upper edges. Lock the lid onto the pot.

2.

Set the machine for	Set the level for	The valve must be	And set the time for	If necessary, press
PRESSURE COOK	MAX	—	20 minutes with the KEEP WARM setting off	START
POULTRY, PRESSURE COOK, or MANUAL	HIGH	Closed	25 minutes with the KEEP WARM setting off	START

3. Use the **quick-release method** to bring the pot's pressure back to normal. Unlatch the lid and open the cooker. Use the edge of a large, metal spoon and a meat fork to break the ground turkey into tiny bits.

4.

Press the button for	Set it for	Set the time for	If necessary, press
SAUTÉ	MEDIUM, NORMAL, or CUSTOM 400°F	5 minutes	START

5. Bring the turkey mixture to a simmer, stirring quite often. Stir in the cornmeal and simmer until thickened, 2–3 minutes. Turn off the SAUTÉ function, set the lid askew over the pot, and set aside for 5 minutes to thicken some more. Serve warm in tortillas with shredded lettuce and cheese.

 Using a **–20°F CHEST FREEZER?** There is no difference in cooking times.

Beyond

- For an **8-quart Instant Pot,** you must increase the broth to 1 cup.

- Go beyond our serving suggestions: Add sliced radishes, thinly sliced red onion, sprouts (particularly radish sprouts), sour cream, and/or sliced pickled jalapeño rings to your taco.

- Use the turkey taco filling (without the tortillas or lettuce) to stuff omelets on the weekend. Or serve it warm with a fried or poached egg on top. Don't forget to top with grated cheese.

- If you use this taco filling for burritos, make sure you drain it, especially if you intend to wrap those burritos up and eat them by hand at lunch.

Turkey Green Chili

6–8 servings

One 16-ounce jar green salsa or tomatillo sauce (2 cups)

1 cup chicken broth

8 ounces (2 to 2½ cups) frozen unseasoned mixed vegetables, preferably a blend with corn

One 15-ounce can white beans, drained and rinsed (1¾ cups)

½ cup frozen chopped onion; or 1 small yellow or white onion, peeled and chopped

One 4½-ounce can chopped mild or hot green chiles (½ cup)

1 tablespoon ground cumin

1 tablespoon stemmed and minced fresh oregano leaves, or 2 teaspoons dried oregano

Two 1-pound packages frozen ground turkey

Because a green chili doesn't include tomatoes, it's super easy to make with jarred green salsa or tomatillo sauce. The flavors are bright and citrusy, so much so that we think the chili is better on a summer evening with a cold pilsner than on a winter night with a glass of red wine. Green chili also goes really well with warm cornbread, even purchased cornbread muffins. As in the recipe for Turkey Tacos, you *must* use two 1-pound packages of ground turkey, not one 2-pound package.

1. Stir the salsa, broth, vegetables, beans, onion, chiles, cumin, and oregano in a **6- or 8-quart Instant Pot.** Set the two blocks of frozen turkey in the pot so that they look like an A-frame or a lean-to, sticking up out of the liquid and balancing against each other along their tops. Lock the lid onto the pot.

2.

Set the machine for	Set the level for	The valve must be	And set the time for	If necessary, press
PRESSURE COOK	MAX	—	20 minutes with the KEEP WARM setting off	START
BEAN/CHILI, PRESSURE COOK, or MANUAL	HIGH	Closed	25 minutes with the KEEP WARM setting off	START

3. Use the **quick-release method** to bring the pot's pressure back to normal. Unlatch the lid and open the cooker. Use the edge of a large, metal spoon and a meat fork to break the ground turkey into tiny bits, even some shreds. Stir well and serve hot.

Using a **-20°F CHEST FREEZER?** There is no difference in cooking times.

Beyond

- Garnish the chili with sour cream or shredded Monterey Jack, or even a shredded Tex-Mex blend.

- Make a jalapeño salsa fresca to go on top. Stem, seed, and mince 2 medium fresh jalapeño chiles. Stir together with 3 tablespoons minced cherry tomatoes, 1 tablespoon minced red onion, 1 tablespoon stemmed and minced cilantro leaves, 1 tablespoon vegetable or olive oil, 1½ teaspoons red wine vinegar, and ¼ teaspoon table salt. Spoon this salsa fresca over each serving.

Turkey and Sweet Potato Hash

4 servings

1 cup chicken broth

1 pound <u>frozen</u> ground turkey

1 cup <u>frozen</u> chopped onion; or 1 medium yellow or white onion, peeled and chopped

¾ cup thinly sliced celery (about 3 medium stalks)

2 teaspoons stemmed and minced fresh sage leaves, or 1 teaspoon dried sage

1 teaspoon onion powder

½ teaspoon fennel seeds

½ teaspoon salt

One 20-ounce bag <u>frozen</u> sweet potato tots or puffs

4 tablespoons (½ stick) butter, cut into bits

There's no way to categorize this dish. Breakfast? Lunch? Dinner? It's got the flavors of a sausage hash (sage and fennel), but it's not very savory with all those sweet potatoes. In the end, we decided it was just pure comfort food, ready in no time.

You'll note the technique here is a little different from other recipes with ground turkey. You have to remove the block of frozen turkey from the cooker, then chop it up on a cutting board. We've added that step because we remove most of the liquid in the cooker — and you have to get the turkey out of the pot to do that. Once the ground turkey is out of the pot, you might as well chop it into little bits for the best texture.

1. Pour the broth into a **6-quart Instant Pot.** Set the pot's rack (with the handles up) or a large, open vegetable steamer inside the pot. Set the frozen block of ground turkey on the rack or in the steamer. Lock the lid onto the pot.

2.

Set the machine for	Set the level for	The valve must be	And set the time for	If necessary, press
PRESSURE COOK	MAX	—	17 minutes with the KEEP WARM setting off	START
POULTRY, PRESSURE COOK, or MANUAL	HIGH	Closed	20 minutes with the KEEP WARM setting off	START

3. Use the **quick-release method** to bring the pot's pressure back to normal. Unlatch the lid and open the cooker. Use kitchen tongs to transfer the block of ground turkey to a nearby cutting board. Remove the rack or steamer from the cooker. Save 1 cup of liquid from the cooker and pour out the rest.

4. Chop the ground turkey into small bits with a large chef's knife. Scrape the turkey back into the pot, then add the onion, celery, sage, onion powder, fennel seeds, and salt. Stir well.

5. Sprinkle the frozen sweet potato tots or puffs over the other ingredients, then pour the reserved 1 cup of broth over the tots. Sprinkle the butter bits on top and lock the lid onto the pot.

6.

Set the machine for	Set the level for	The valve must be	And set the time for	If necessary, press
PRESSURE COOK	MAX	—	2 minutes with the KEEP WARM setting off	START
POULTRY, PRESSURE COOK, or MANUAL	HIGH	Closed	3 minutes with the KEEP WARM setting off	START

7. Use the **quick-release method** again to bring the pot's pressure back to normal. Unlatch the lid and open the cooker. To serve, scoop into bowls, keeping some of the sweet potato tots or puffs intact.

Beyond

- For an **8-quart Instant Pot,** you must increase all the ingredients by 50 percent. If you can't find a ½-pound package of ground turkey, use 1 pound of frozen ground turkey and double the onion and celery.

- Make a heartier meal by setting a poached or fried egg on top of each serving.

- Garnish the hash with plenty of ground black pepper and maybe a dash of hot red pepper sauce, either sriracha or Frank's RedHot.

 Using a **-20°F CHEST FREEZER?** There is no difference in cooking times.

Chinatown-Style Chop Suey with Ground Turkey

4 servings

¾ cup chicken broth

3 tablespoons regular or reduced-sodium soy sauce or tamari

3 tablespoons unseasoned rice vinegar (see headnote on page 92); or 2 tablespoons apple cider vinegar

1 teaspoon ground dried ginger

1 pound <u>frozen</u> ground turkey

1½ pounds (6 cups) <u>frozen</u> unseasoned mixed vegetables for stir-fry (any seasoning packet discarded)

2 tablespoons water

1½ tablespoons cornstarch

Crunchy chow mein noodles (gluten-free, if that's a concern), for garnish

Here's the mid-century-modern classic that has little in common with authentic Chinese fare but was a staple of the American table for years. We've used ground turkey, instead of ground pork or beef, because we feel the others made the dish too greasy. For an all-American take on chop suey, see the pasta dish on pages 58–59.

1. Stir the broth, soy sauce or tamari, vinegar, and ground ginger in a **6-quart Instant Pot.** Set the pot's rack (with the handles up) or a large, open vegetable steamer inside the pot. Set the block of frozen ground turkey on the rack or in the steamer. Lock the lid onto the pot.

2.

Set the machine for	Set the level for	The valve must be	And set the time for	If necessary, press
PRESSURE COOK	MAX	—	17 minutes with the KEEP WARM setting off	START
POULTRY, PRESSURE COOK, or MANUAL	HIGH	Closed	20 minutes with the KEEP WARM setting off	START

3. Use the **quick-release method** to bring the pot's pressure back to normal. Unlatch the lid and open the cooker. Remove the rack or steamer from the cooker, letting the block of ground turkey fall in the liquid. Break up the ground turkey with the edge of a large, metal spoon and a meat fork, getting it into small pieces (rather than longish threads). Place the vegetables on top of the meat but do not stir them into the ingredients below. Lock the lid back on.

4.

Set the machine for	Set the level for	The valve must be	And set the time for	If necessary, press
POULTRY, PRESSURE COOK, or MANUAL	HIGH	Closed	0 minutes (see page 163) with the KEEP WARM setting off	START

5. Again, use the **quick-release method** to bring the pot's pressure back to normal. Unlatch the lid and open the pot again. Whisk the water and cornstarch in a small bowl until smooth.

6.

Press the button for	Set it for	Set the time for	If necessary, press
SAUTÉ	MEDIUM, NORMAL, or CUSTOM 400°F	5 minutes	START

7. Bring the contents of the cooker to a simmer, stirring often. Stir in the cornstarch slurry, then continue cooking, stirring almost constantly, until the liquid thickens, about 1 minute. Turn off the SAUTÉ function and remove the (hot!) insert from the pot to stop the cooking. Set aside for a couple of minutes to continue to thicken. Stir well and serve warm with the crunchy chow mein noodles sprinkled over the top.

Beyond

- For an **8-quart Instant Pot,** you must increase all the ingredients by 50 percent. (If you can't find ½ pound frozen turkey, keep the ground turkey at 1 pound and double the amount of frozen vegetables.)

- Although this dish's roots lie in Cantonese-American restaurants, a drizzle of sriracha or Asian red chile sauce wouldn't hurt!

 Using a **–20°F CHEST FREEZER?** There is no difference in cooking times.

Turkey Meatballs with Buttery Rice Pilaf

4 servings

2½ cups chicken broth

1 cup plus 1 tablespoon raw white basmati rice (see page 9)

½ cup <u>frozen</u> chopped onion; or 1 small yellow or white onion, peeled and chopped

2 teaspoons stemmed and minced fresh sage leaves, or 1 teaspoon dried sage

1 teaspoon stemmed fresh thyme leaves, or ½ teaspoon dried thyme

½ teaspoon table salt

1½ pounds <u>frozen</u> mini or bite-sized turkey meatballs (a gluten-free version, if that's a concern), ½ to 1 ounce each

2 tablespoons butter

Here's a great one-pot casserole for whenever time's tight. Note that you must heat the liquid in the cooker before you add the frozen meatballs. Otherwise, they'll drop the temperature of the liquid too low, the rice will fall to the bottom of the pot before it can come to pressure, and you'll end up with a burn notice.

1.

Press the button for	Set it for	Set the time for	If necessary, press
SAUTÉ	HIGH, MORE, or CUSTOM 400°F	10 minutes	START

2. Mix the broth, rice, onion, sage, thyme, and salt in a **6-quart Instant Pot.** Cook, stirring occasionally, until many wisps of steam rise from the liquid. Stir in the frozen meatballs, then turn off the SAUTÉ function. Set the butter in the mixture and lock the lid onto the pot.

3.

Set the machine for	Set the level for	The valve must be	And set the time for	If necessary, press
PRESSURE COOK	MAX	—	10 minutes with the KEEP WARM setting off	START
POULTRY, PRESSURE COOK, or MANUAL	HIGH	Closed	12 minutes with the KEEP WARM setting off	START

4. Use the **quick-release method** to bring the pot's pressure back to normal — but *do not open the lid*. Leave the pot undisturbed for 10 minutes after the pressure has been released. Unlatch the lid and open the cooker. Stir well before serving.

Beyond

- For an **8-quart Instant Pot,** you must increase all the ingredients by 50 percent.

- Swap out the herbs for any you prefer. We've skewed these to match the Italian flavoring in most meatballs. But if you've got plain meatballs, try a mix of dried thyme and dried dill, or even stemmed and minced fresh parsley and tarragon leaves.

- Cheese is a welcome garnish, particularly finely grated Parmigiano-Reggiano or another hard, aged cheese.

 Using a **-20°F CHEST FREEZER?** There is no difference in cooking times.

Road Map: **Roast Turkey Breast**

6–8 servings

1 cup liquid

Choose from water, broth, white wine of any sort, light-colored beer of any sort, unsweetened apple juice, or a 50-50 combo of any of these.

One 6-pound <u>frozen</u> bone-in skin-on turkey breast

Nonstick spray of any flavor (but *not* baking spray)

1½ tablespoons dried seasoning blend

Choose from Provençal, Italian, za'atar, Tex-Mex, chili seasoning, or any you prefer or can create.

1 teaspoon table salt, optional (check to see if the seasoning blend includes salt)

Yes, you can cook a whole turkey breast in an Instant Pot. True, it's not *roasted* in any sense of the word, but the flavor is like the best roast turkey breast, moist and tender.

Problem is, you can cook the cut *only* in an **8-quart model** because of the size of the breast. So here's the one and only recipe in this book that skips over the **6-quart pot.** Hey, listen, you can make a fine "roast" chicken in a 6-quart pot from a frozen chicken (pages 78–79). But this one recipe might be a reason to get a larger pot. Haven't you always thought, "I've got a holiday ham but I wish I had turkey breast, too"? We certainly have.

You may think there's too little liquid to make steam in an 8-quart cooker. Don't worry: The turkey breast will give off plenty more liquid as it thaws.

1. Pour the liquid into an **8-quart Instant Pot.** Spray the turkey breast all over with nonstick spray, then lightly coat it (particularly the skin) with the dried seasoning blend and salt (if using). Set it in the pot and lock on the lid.

2.

Set the machine for	Set the level for	The valve must be	And set the time for	If necessary, press
PRESSURE COOK	MAX	—	1 hour 12 minutes with the KEEP WARM setting off	START
POULTRY, PRESSURE COOK, or MANUAL	HIGH	Closed	1 hour 20 minutes with the KEEP WARM setting off	START

3. When the machine has finished cooking, turn it off and let its pressure **return to normal naturally,** about 35 minutes. Unlatch the lid and open the cooker. Insert an instant-read meat thermometer into the thickest part of the breast without touching bone. It must register at least 165°F. If it doesn't, lock the lid back on the pot and give it 10 more minutes at MAX or HIGH followed by a **quick release.** Use kitchen tongs, a large metal spatula, and deft coordination to transfer the turkey breast to a nearby cutting board. Cool for 10 minutes before slicing.

Beyond

- You'll end up with some pretty terrific turkey stock in the pot. Don't waste it!

- If you want to brown and crisp the skin, set a rack about 10 inches from the broiler and heat the broiler. Set the cooked turkey breast skin-side up on a lipped baking sheet. Broil the top until browned, about 2 minutes, then turn the breast and broil on each side until browned, about 1 minute each.

 Using a **-20°F CHEST FREEZER?** Cook under pressure in step 2 for 1 hour 30 minutes on the MAX setting, or for 1 hour 40 minutes on the HIGH setting, followed by a **natural release.**

4

Beef

When we started writing this book, we assumed this chapter would be the biggest, what with all the possibilities for frozen ground beef. But as we began experimenting with what the pot can do, we found that the sun doesn't rise and set on hamburger meat. The other chapters then expanded because there was so much to do with, say, frozen chicken breasts or frozen shrimp.

But beef may still be the heart of this book. It is such a natural in the pot because it cooks evenly, is forgiving (especially in stews and braises), and gets so tasty as the pot blends beef's natural flavors with herbs, spices, and tomatoes.

There are no esoteric cuts in this chapter: no oxtails, beef cheeks, or skirt steak. We felt these cuts involved a bit more effort than a book devoted to what's essentially pantry cooking. This chapter uses ground beef, beef stew meat, and chuck roast. There are also a few recipes for round and flank steaks and one for short ribs.

These recipes were tested with both standard *and* grass-fed beef. We found no difference in the timings for ground beef. We found that the larger grass-fed cuts (like a chuck roast or short ribs) often needed an extra 5 to 10 minutes under pressure. But (sigh) not always. "Grass-fed" is a marker for a wide range of variables. It's best to use our suggested timing and then check.

One warning about self-defrosting freezers before you get started: No cut of beef can stay indefinitely in a self-defrosting freezer that comes up near 32°F every once in a while to melt any ice crystals. Unfortunately, those temperature fluctuations cause those very crystals to form in the meat, leading to freezer burn and tough bits at the edges. Consider three months your marker for how long you can keep beef in a standard, 0°F freezer (maybe six months in a chest freezer without a self-defrosting function).

Road Map: **Burgers**

Up to 6 servings

1½ cups water

For the Burgers

One 10-inch-long piece of aluminum foil

One 6-ounce <u>frozen</u> burger patty

Table salt and ground black pepper, to taste

Optional Add-Ons

1 thin slice semi-firm cheese, such as Cheddar, Swiss, mozzarella, Monterey Jack, Colby, Gruyère, or American cheese

1 brown or white mushroom, thinly sliced

2 tablespoons <u>frozen</u> chopped onion or peeled and chopped yellow or white onion

Up to 4 thin fresh jalapeño slices

Up to 1 tablespoon butter

Up to ¼ teaspoon dried seasoning blend (omit the salt on the patties if there's salt in the blend)

Up to ¼ teaspoon peeled and minced garlic

This recipe lets you customize as many burgers as you like. You can make each patty plain, or you can add any number of toppings before wrapping them up in aluminum foil. Why do we wrap the frozen patties and not just set them on the rack in the pot? Because the juices stay with the burgers, rather than running into the water below, giving the patties a much "beefier" flavor.

Notice that you must make your own patties, ones that are larger than the standard, 3- or 4-ounce burgers sometimes sold frozen in boxes. We find that those smaller patties cook too quickly and dry out in the Instant Pot. (They're best for the grill, even when still frozen.)

You can prepare the patties for this recipe far in advance — if, say, you've bought fresh ground beef ahead of time. Make 6-ounce patties that are about ½ inch thick and add the toppings of your choice (if any). Wrap each patty individually and store them in the freezer for several months. And one more thing: Label them so you'll know which patty has which toppings (if any).

You can make beef and pork burgers with a 50-50 combo of ground beef and ground pork. We recommend using lean ground beef to go with the fattier ground pork. But do cook these patties following the "no pink" instructions (for food safety reasons).

1. Pour the water into a **6- or 8-quart Instant Pot.** Set the pot's rack (with the handles up) or a large, open vegetable steamer inside the pot.

2. Set the foil sheet on your work surface with one long side facing you. Set the frozen patty in the middle of the sheet and season with salt and pepper. If desired, set one, a few, or many add-ons on the patty (smearing the condiments over the meat). Fold over the foil's short sides until they meet in the middle, then crimp them closed. Also crimp closed the seam along both sides of the foil packet, folding the ends up (not down), so that the juices in the packet won't run out. Repeat to make up to 6 patties. Set the patties on the rack or in the steamer, overlapping where necessary without stacking them on top of each other (and also without any being placed vertical in the pot). Lock the lid onto the cooker.

3.

Set the machine for	Set the level for	The valve must be	And set the time for	If necessary, press
PRESSURE COOK	MAX	—	20 minutes for a pink burger, or 25 minutes for a no-pink burger (both with the KEEP WARM setting off)	START
MEAT/ STEW, PRESSURE COOK, or MANUAL	HIGH	Closed	25 minutes for a pink burger, or 30 minutes for a no-pink burger (both with the KEEP WARM setting off)	START

4. If you've used the MAX pressure setting: For a pink burger, when the machine has finished cooking (20 minutes), use the **quick-release method** to return the pot's pressure to normal. For a no-pink burger, turn the machine off when it's finished cooking (25 minutes) and let it **return to normal pressure** for 5 minutes, then use the **quick-release method** to get rid of the remaining pressure.

   If you've used the HIGH pressure setting: For a pink burger, turn the machine off when it has finished cooking (25 minutes) and let the pressure **return to normal naturally** for 5 minutes. For a no-pink burger, turn the machine off when it has finished cooking (30 minutes) and let the pressure **return to normal naturally** for 10 minutes. *In both cases,* then use the **quick-release method** to get rid of any remaining pressure.

5. Unlatch the lid and open the cooker. Use tongs and a large metal spatula to remove the wrapped patties one by one from the cooker. Unwrap them carefully (they're super hot), then use the spatula to transfer them to serving plates.

 Using a **-20°F CHEST FREEZER?** There is no difference in cooking times.

Beyond

- You can fit up to 10 wrapped burgers in an **8-quart Instant Pot.**

- Of course, you can garnish your burgers with lettuce and sliced tomato. And maybe a thin slice of red onion, too, if they hadn't already been topped with chopped onions before cooking. But you can also go far beyond the norm. Try kimchi and mayonnaise (our personal favorite), sauerkraut and deli mustard, pickled jalapeño rings and barbecue sauce, or tapenade and Dijon mustard.

- Don't stand on ceremony with hamburger buns. Consider kaiser rolls, toasted English muffins, or even thick slices of Texas toast.

- Note that there are no acidic condiments among the add-ons, like chutney, pickle relish, India relish, chowchow, kimchi, ketchup, or Dijon mustard. These can react with the foil as the burger cooks. If you want any (or all?) of them, add them after cooking, or lay a sheet of parchment paper on top of the patty and condiments before wrapping it in foil so the acidic condiments never touch the aluminum.

Road Map: **Pot Pie**

4 servings

For the Stew

2 cups broth of any sort

1 tablespoon Worcestershire sauce

1 pound <u>frozen</u> ground meat

Choose from beef, buffalo, venison, pork, turkey, chicken, or even sausage meat — or a combo of any two you prefer.

2 teaspoons dried seasoning blend

Choose either a prepared seasoning such as Italian or Tex-Mex or a blend you create (rosemary, oregano, thyme, parsley, and basil are the norms, but enhance them with a little ground allspice or grated nutmeg).

½ teaspoon table salt, optional (check to see if the seasoning blend includes salt)

½ teaspoon ground black pepper

1 pound (4 to 5 cups) <u>frozen</u> unseasoned mixed vegetables

Choose from any unseasoned blend, so long as you omit any flavoring packets. Or use a combination of frozen corn kernels, bell pepper strips, chopped onion, and/or sliced carrots.

½ cup heavy or light cream (but not "fat-free" cream)

2½ tablespoons all-purpose flour

Here's one recipe with dozens of ways to make pot pie using frozen meat and vegetables in the cooker. Admittedly, the process is a tad complicated. First, you steam the frozen meat until thawed and partially ready, then you add frozen vegetables and heat them to simmering before thickening the sauce. Finally, you make a drop-biscuit dough and use the pot's SLOW COOK function to create the topping. See? It's all a fair amount of work. But worth it, for sure.

The drop biscuits can be sprinkled with cheese, but they should be sprinkled with paprika no matter what. The little dumplings won't brown in the pot and the paprika gives them a more appealing appearance.

1. To make the stew, pour the broth and Worcestershire sauce into a **6- or 8-quart Instant Pot.** Set the pot's rack (with the handles up) or a large, open vegetable steamer inside the pot. Set the ground meat on the rack or in the steamer. Sprinkle the seasoning blend, salt (if using), and pepper over the meat. Lock the lid onto the pot.

2.

Set the machine for	Set the level for	The valve must be	And set the time for	If necessary, press
PRESSURE COOK	MAX	—	18 minutes with the KEEP WARM setting off	START
MEAT/STEW, PRESSURE COOK, or MANUAL	HIGH	Closed	20 minutes with the KEEP WARM setting off	START

3. Use the **quick-release method** to bring the pot's pressure back to normal. Unlatch the lid and open the cooker. Use silicone cooking mitts or thick hot pads to remove the rack or steamer, letting the meat fall down into the liquid below. Use the edge of a large, metal spoon and a meat fork to break the meat up into little chunks, about the size of very small meatballs. Stir in the frozen vegetables.

4.

Press the button for	Set it for	Set the time for	If necessary, press
SAUTÉ	HIGH, MORE, or CUSTOM 400°F	5 minutes	START

5. Whisk the cream and flour in a small bowl until smooth. Once the liquid is simmering in the pot, add this cream mixture and whisk until bubbling. Turn off the SAUTÉ function.

6. To make the biscuit topping, stir the flour, baking powder, and salt in a medium bowl until uniform. Add the milk, melted butter or oil, and the egg. Continue stirring until the mixture has no dry ingredients in the bottom of the bowl.

RECIPE CONTINUES

For the Biscuit Topping

1¼ cups all-purpose flour

1½ teaspoons baking powder

½ teaspoon table salt

6 tablespoons whole or low-fat milk

1 tablespoon butter, melted and cooled; or 1 tablespoon oil of any sort you prefer

1 large egg

4 ounces (1 cup) shredded semi-firm cheese, such as Cheddar, Swiss, or even a prepared blend, optional

½ teaspoon mild paprika

Beyond

- For a simpler recipe, there's no need to make your own drop biscuits. Instead, set eight of the ten or so biscuits from a 10-ounce can right on top of the stew, top them with cheese (if you want) and paprika, then cook with the SLOW COOK function as directed.

- If you want to make your own dried seasoning blend, try ½ teaspoon dried sage, ½ teaspoon dried thyme, ½ teaspoon garlic powder, and ½ teaspoon onion powder. Or experiment with a blend of all sorts of dried herbs and even spices (thyme, parsley, and cinnamon make a good grouping). Use only dried herbs, not fresh. The fresh don't add quite the punch to this long, involved cooking process.

7. Drop the mixture by eight blobs on top of the hot stew. Sprinkle the cheese (if using) over each of the blobs, then sprinkle each with a little paprika. Latch the lid onto the pot but do not engage the pressure valve.

8.

Set the machine for	Set the level for	The valve must be	And set the time for	If necessary, press
SLOW COOK	HIGH	Open	30 minutes with the KEEP WARM setting off	START

9. When the machine has finished cooking, turn it off and open the lid. Cool for a few minutes, then use a large cooking spoon to scoop the biscuits and stew into serving bowls.

❄ Using a **–20°F CHEST FREEZER?** There is no difference in cooking times.

French Dip Sandwiches

4–6 servings

An old-school diner sandwich, a French dip is really only as good as the bread it's made with — which should be a baguette or a narrow French loaf that is decidedly crunchy, not soft and gummy. If the baguette is soft, put it in a 300°F oven for perhaps 10 minutes to get it crisp. That way, it'll stand up to the "dip" (the pan juices) without becoming soggy.

There's a slight chance the cooked beef might still be pink inside, depending on the thickness and density of the frozen shaved beef. If the meat is pink, turn the pot to HIGH on its SAUTÉ function after cooking under pressure and breaking up the beef. Cook, stirring often, until the meat is cooked through, about 2 minutes.

1. Stir the broth, onion, thyme, onion powder, garlic powder, salt, and pepper in a **6- or 8-quart Instant Pot.** Set the frozen block of meat in the liquid and lock the lid onto the pot.

2.

Set the machine for	Set the level for	The valve must be	And set the time for	If necessary, press
PRESSURE COOK	MAX	—	8 minutes with the KEEP WARM setting off	START
MEAT/STEW, PRESSURE COOK, or MANUAL	HIGH	Closed	10 minutes with the KEEP WARM setting off	START

3. Use the **quick-release method** to bring the pot's pressure back to normal. Unlatch the lid and open the cooker. Use the edge of a large, metal spoon and a meat fork to break the meat into chips and strips.

4. Lightly butter the inside of the baguette slices. Use tongs to transfer the strips of meat to the buns to make sandwiches. Pour the (hot!) liquid from the cooker into a serving bowl or small soup bowls. Use this broth as a dip for the sandwiches.

3 cups beef or chicken broth

½ cup frozen chopped onion; or 1 small yellow or white onion, peeled and chopped

Up to 1 tablespoon stemmed thyme leaves, or 1½ teaspoons dried thyme

1 teaspoon onion powder

1 teaspoon garlic powder

½ teaspoon table salt

½ teaspoon ground black pepper

2 pounds frozen shaved beef

Butter, for the sandwiches

A French baguette (gluten-free, if that is a concern), cut into 4- to 6-inch lengths, each sliced open lengthwise

Beyond

- To simplify this recipe, substitute three 9-ounce boxes of frozen Steak-umm sliced steaks for the shaved beef. Break each Steak-umm sheet into three or four long strips. Cook these at MAX for 1 minute or at HIGH for 2 minutes with a QUICK RELEASE.

- For a more sweet-and-sour flavor, add up to 2 tablespoons steak sauce (such as A.1.) and 1 teaspoon granulated sugar to the broth in step 1.

Using a **-20°F CHEST FREEZER?** There is no difference in cooking times.

Sloppy Joes

4–6 servings

½ cup beef or chicken broth

2 tablespoons regular or reduced-sodium soy sauce or tamari

1 tablespoon Worcestershire sauce (gluten-free, if that is a concern)

1 tablespoon light brown sugar

4 ounces (1 cup) <u>frozen</u> bell pepper strips

½ cup <u>frozen</u> chopped onion

1 teaspoon peeled and minced garlic

1 pound <u>frozen</u> ground beef

½ cup ketchup

2 teaspoons prepared yellow mustard

2 tablespoons tomato paste

Hamburger buns or kaiser rolls (gluten-free, if that is a concern), for serving

This sloppy joe filling isn't too sweet, with just a little brown sugar to bring out the salty condiments in the sauce. But be careful: It can get really salty, particularly because of the Worcestershire sauce. We recommend using reduced-sodium alternatives where possible for the ketchup, mustard, and tomato paste.

You'll notice that the recipe calls for very little broth and for *only* <u>frozen</u> bell pepper strips and <u>frozen</u> chopped onion, *without their fresh alternatives*. These frozen items will release plenty of moisture as they thaw and cook, more moisture than their fresh versions would—and so we needn't swamp the pot with extra liquid (which would result in a soupier sloppy joe filling, hardly suitable for buns).

1. Stir the broth, soy sauce or tamari, Worcestershire sauce, and brown sugar in a **6-quart Instant Pot** until the brown sugar dissolves. Stir in the bell pepper strips, onion, and garlic. Set the lump of frozen ground beef in the sauce, then put the ketchup and mustard on top of the beef. Lock the lid onto the cooker.

2.

Set the machine for	Set the level for	The valve must be	And set the time for	If necessary, press
PRESSURE COOK	MAX	—	15 minutes with the KEEP WARM setting off	START
MEAT/STEW, PRESSURE COOK, or MANUAL	HIGH	Closed	20 minutes with the KEEP WARM setting off	START

3. Use the **quick-release method** to bring the pot's pressure back to normal. Unlatch the lid and open the cooker. Use the edge of a large, metal spoon and a meat fork to break the meat into tiny, chewy bits, not quite threads but smaller than mini meatballs. (Note: Although the meat will still be pink or red inside, it will cook more in the next steps.)

4.

Press the button for	Set it for	Set the time for	If necessary, press
SAUTÉ	HIGH, MORE, or CUSTOM 400°F	5 minutes	START

5. Stir in the tomato paste as the ingredients come to a simmer in the pot. Cook at a simmer, stirring often, until somewhat thickened, about 2 minutes. Turn off the SAUTÉ function and set the lid askew over the pot. Set aside for a couple of minutes, just to let the filling continue to thicken. Serve the warm filling on split-open buns or rolls.

 Using a **−20°F CHEST FREEZER?** There is no difference in cooking times.

Beyond

- For an **8-quart Instant Pot,** you must increase the ingredients by 50 percent (or double them).

- Make the filling richer by adding up to 3 tablespoons butter with the brown sugar.

- And/or substitute beef broth for the water.

- Toast the buns: Spread a little butter or olive oil on the cut sides, then toast cut-side up on a lipped baking sheet about 4 inches from a heated broiler — or toast them cut-side down in a skillet set over medium heat.

- Condiments matter on the buns! Our favorites are chowchow, pickled onions, pickled jalapeño rings, dill pickle sandwich slices, and/or coleslaw.

- Sloppy joe filling makes a new take on nachos: Spread a little over tortilla chips on a large, lipped baking sheet, add shredded cheese, and broil until bubbling and lightly brown.

All-American Chili

6–8 servings

One 28-ounce can diced
  tomatoes packed in juice
  (3½ cups)

Two 15-ounce cans red kidney
  beans, drained and rinsed
  (3½ cups total)

One 16-ounce jar chunky-style
  mild or hot red salsa (about
  2 cups)

1 cup beef or chicken broth

1 cup frozen chopped onion; or
  1 small yellow or white onion,
  peeled and chopped

One 4½-ounce can chopped
  mild or hot green chiles
  (½ cup)

¼ cup standard chili powder

Two frozen 1-pound blocks of
  ground beef

This fast, well-stocked chili makes a lot, so be prepared to have plenty of leftovers, particularly good for lunch or spooned over cheese omelets for a hearty weekend breakfast. The leftovers can also be frozen in a sealed container for a fast meal in the weeks ahead.

Because of the way the frozen meat cooks in the liquid, you must use two 1-pound frozen blocks of ground beef, *not* one 2-pound lump.

1.

Press the button for	Set it for	Set the time for	If necessary, press
SAUTÉ	HIGH, MORE, or CUSTOM 400°F	10 minutes	START

2. Mix the tomatoes, beans, salsa, broth, onion, chiles, and chili powder in a **6- or 8-quart Instant Pot.** Cook, stirring often, until many wisps of steam rise from the liquid. (It's important to get the liquid hot because there are *two* blocks of frozen ground beef.) Turn off the SAUTÉ function and stand the ground beef in the sauce so that the two pieces lean against each other like an A-frame. Lock the lid onto the pot.

3.

Set the machine for	Set the level for	The valve must be	And set the time for	If necessary, press
PRESSURE COOK	MAX	—	18 minutes with the KEEP WARM setting off	START
BEAN/CHILI, PRESSURE COOK, or MANUAL	HIGH	Closed	20 minutes with the KEEP WARM setting off	START

4. Use the **quick-release method** to bring the pot's pressure back to normal. Unlatch the lid and open the cooker. Use tongs and a slotted spoon to transfer the two blocks of meat to a nearby large cutting board. (If you don't have a cutting board large enough, handle the meat blocks one at a time.)

5.

Press the button for	Set it for	Set the time for	If necessary, press
SAUTÉ	HIGH, MORE, or CUSTOM 400°F	5 minutes	START

6. As the sauce comes to a simmer in the cooker, use a meat fork and a large knife to chop the ground beef into fairly small bits, certainly smaller than mini meatballs, even down to ground beef shreds. Stir these (and any juices on the board) back into the cooker. Cook, stirring all the while, for 1 minute. Turn off the SAUTÉ function and set the chili aside for a couple of minutes to blend the flavors before serving hot.

 Using a **-20°F CHEST FREEZER?** There is no difference in cooking times.

Beyond

- You can halve this recipe in a **6-quart Instant Pot.** In this case, set the lump of ground beef directly in the warmed liquid and other ingredients.

- For more flavor, add any or all of the following to the cooker with the chili powder: up to 1 tablespoon dried oregano, up to 2 teaspoons ground cinnamon, up to 1 teaspoon ground cumin, and/or up to 1 teaspoon red pepper flakes.

- Garnish the chili with shredded cheese (particularly sharp Cheddar), sour cream, and pickled jalapeño rings.

- Make chili pie by serving the hot chili over Fritos, then topping it with shredded American cheese and a little minced red onion.

Meatball Chili

6 servings

One 24-ounce jar chunky-style mild or hot red salsa (3 cups)

Two 15-ounce cans white, black, or navy beans, drained and rinsed (3½ cups total)

2 cups beef, chicken, or vegetable broth

8 ounces (2 cups) frozen bell pepper strips; or 2 medium red or green bell peppers, stemmed, cored, and cut into thin strips

¼ cup chili powder

1 teaspoon ground cumin

½ teaspoon table salt

One 25-ounce bag frozen mini or bite-sized meatballs (even vegan and/or gluten-free if that's a concern), ½ to 1 ounce each

One 6-ounce can tomato paste (⅔ cup)

Dinner can't get much easier! You can use this recipe as a road map of sorts. Vary the salsa (maybe even a green salsa?) and the type of meatballs. We tested this with Italian-style meatballs, but there are lots of other varieties on the market.

And it needn't be beef meatballs. Consider turkey, even buffalo. Or make a vegan chili with vegan meatballs and vegetable broth. The only trick is to use frozen mini meatballs.

1.

Press the button for	Set it for	Set the time for	If necessary, press
SAUTÉ	HIGH, MORE, or CUSTOM 400°F	10 minutes	START

2. Mix the salsa, beans, broth, bell pepper strips, chili powder, cumin, and salt in a **6- or 8-quart Instant Pot.** Cook, stirring often, until many wisps of steam rise from the liquid. Turn off the SAUTÉ function and stir in the meatballs. Lock the lid onto the cooker.

3.

Set the machine for	Set the level for	The valve must be	And set the time for	If necessary, press
PRESSURE COOK	MAX	—	5 minutes with the KEEP WARM setting off	START
BEAN/CHILI, PRESSURE COOK, or MANUAL	HIGH	Closed	8 minutes with the KEEP WARM setting off	START

4. Use the **quick-release method** to bring the pot's pressure back to normal. Unlatch the lid and open the cooker.

5.

Press the button for	Set it for	Set the time for	If necessary, press
SAUTÉ	HIGH, MORE, or CUSTOM 400°F	5 minutes	START

6. As the chili comes to a simmer, stir in the tomato paste until smooth. Continue cooking, stirring often, until somewhat thickened, 1–2 minutes. Turn off the SAUTÉ function and set aside for 5 minutes to continue to blend the flavors and help the chili to set up.

 Using a **–20°F CHEST FREEZER?** There is no difference in cooking times.

Beyond

- Of all the chilis in this book, this one calls out most to be served over cooked, long-grain, white rice.

- Or go all out and serve it over cooked buckwheat (not kasha, but dried, plain buckwheat).

- Garnish the servings with sour cream, pickled jalapeño rings, minced fresh jalapeño, minced red onion, pickled onions, and/or shredded cheese, particularly sharp Cheddar.

Middle Eastern–Inspired Beef and Rice Casserole

4–6 servings

1½ cups beef or chicken broth

1 cup <u>frozen</u> chopped onion; or 1 medium yellow or white onion, peeled and chopped

1 teaspoon ground coriander

1 teaspoon ground dried ginger

½ teaspoon ground dried turmeric

½ teaspoon ground cinnamon

½ teaspoon table salt

½ teaspoon ground black pepper

2 pounds <u>frozen</u> beef stew meat

1 cup raw white basmati rice (see page 9)

¼ cup sliced almonds

¼ cup raisins

2 tablespoons butter

This beef and rice casserole is a one-pot meal with loads of earthy flavors. Notice that there are two times the casserole goes under pressure: once to cook the beef and then a second time — on HIGH (not MAX) — to cook the rice and finish tenderizing the beef. Don't shortcut these steps, especially the release times after each cooking. The slightly more complicated process will result in a much more satisfying meal that you can pile on a platter and bring to the table to rock that casbah.

1. Mix the broth, onion, coriander, ginger, turmeric, cinnamon, salt, and pepper in a **6- or 8-quart Instant Pot.** Set the beef stew meat in this sauce. Lock the lid onto the cooker.

2.

Set the machine for	Set the level for	The valve must be	And set the time for	If necessary, press
PRESSURE COOK	MAX	—	28 minutes with the KEEP WARM setting off	START
MEAT/STEW, PRESSURE COOK, or MANUAL	HIGH	Closed	35 minutes with the KEEP WARM setting off	START

3. When the machine has finished cooking, turn it off and let its pressure **return to normal naturally,** about 30 minutes. Unlatch the lid and open the cooker. Stir in the rice, almonds, raisins, and butter. Lock the lid back onto the pot.

4.

Set the machine for	Set the level for	The valve must be	And set the time for	If necessary, press
MEAT/STEW, PRESSURE COOK, or MANUAL	HIGH	Closed	12 minutes with the KEEP WARM setting off	START

5. Use the **quick-release method** to bring the pot's pressure back to normal — but *do not open the cooker.* Set aside with the lid on for 10 minutes, then unlatch the lid and open the pot. Stir well before serving warm.

 Using a **-20°F CHEST FREEZER?** There is no difference in cooking times.

Beyond

- For heat, use a hot red pepper sauce like sriracha to garnish each serving.

- And/or garnish the servings with lots of stemmed and minced fresh parsley and/or cilantro leaves.

Unstuffed Cabbage

4–6 servings

One 14-ounce can diced
    tomatoes packed in juice (1⅔
    cups)

1 cup chicken or vegetable broth

2 tablespoons red wine vinegar

2 tablespoons granulated white
    sugar

2 tablespoons raisins

1½ teaspoons mild paprika

1 teaspoon onion powder

½ teaspoon caraway seeds

½ teaspoon table salt

1 small head (1¾ pounds)
    cabbage, cored and chopped
    into ½- to 1-inch pieces (about
    8 cups)

1½ pounds <u>frozen</u> mini or
    bite-sized beef or turkey
    meatballs (or vegan and/or
    gluten-free if that's a
    concern), ½ to 1 ounce each

Consider this a stew version of stuffed cabbage, that comforting Old World braise. With cabbage, beef, tomatoes, and traditional spices, this alternate take has the sweet-and-sour appeal of the original, although it's much easier to make with frozen mini meatballs. Use beef or turkey, but keep in mind the overall flavors of the stew. Plain is best, maybe Italian-seasoned, but not much more exotic than that.

One note: Bagged cabbage won't work with this technique. Shredded, the cabbage will overcook. In fact, the chopped cabbage is put in two layers in the pot so that one layer stays a bit *al dente* or even chewy under pressure.

1. Stir the tomatoes, broth, vinegar, sugar, raisins, paprika, onion powder, caraway seeds, and salt in a **6-quart Instant Pot** until the sugar dissolves.

2. Spread half the chopped cabbage over this liquid mixture, then top that cabbage with the meatballs. Spread the remaining cabbage evenly over the meatballs. Do not stir. Lock the lid onto the pot.

3.

Set the machine for	Set the level for	The valve must be	And set the time for	If necessary, press
PRESSURE COOK	MAX	—	3 minutes with the KEEP WARM setting off	START
MEAT/STEW, PRESSURE COOK, or MANUAL	HIGH	Closed	5 minutes with the KEEP WARM setting off	START

4. Use the **quick-release method** to bring the pot's pressure back to normal. Unlatch the lid and open the cooker. Stir well before serving.

Beyond

- For an **8-quart Instant Pot,** you must increase the broth to 1½ cups.

- Substitute red cabbage for a brightly colored dish.

- If you don't like caraway seeds (or don't want to buy them), substitute ½ teaspoon dried dill.

- For heat, add up to 1 teaspoon red pepper flakes with the spices.

 Using a **-20°F CHEST FREEZER?** There is no difference in cooking times.

Road Map: Beef and Vegetable Stew

6 servings

1 cup liquid

Choose from stock of any sort, wine (preferably white of any sort), dry vermouth, beer of any sort, unsweetened apple cider, or hard cider of any sort, or a combination of two of these.

Up to 3 tablespoons flavor enhancer

Choose from Dijon mustard, yellow mustard, chutney of any sort, barbecue sauce of any sort, ketchup, Worcestershire sauce, regular or reduced-sodium soy sauce, tamari, jarred prepared horseradish, and/or a thick red chili sauce such as Heinz (remembering that some of these are more strongly flavored than others, so you may need less than 3 tablespoons).

½ cup <u>frozen</u> chopped onion; or 1 small yellow or white onion, peeled and chopped

1½ tablespoons dried seasoning blend

Choose from taco seasoning, packaged dry ranch dressing mix, any dried seasoning blend like Italian or Creole, or a dried seasoning blend you concoct.

Up to 2 teaspoons peeled and minced garlic, optional

2½ pounds <u>frozen</u> cubed beef stew meat

This road map may seem a bit complicated: two times under pressure, different releases, only HIGH (not MAX) on the second cooking, then a final sauté to thicken the stew. But the results are worth all that effort. Imagine using frozen beef stew meat to create a warm, comforting meal. *That* seems like a miracle!

Admittedly, because the preparation takes time, this stew is probably best for the weekend since the whole start-to-finish time (with the pot's coming to pressure twice) is close to 1½ hours. Don't despair. Beef stew is a joy from the pot, one of the things the machine does exceptionally well since it helps retain so much moisture in the beef and mellows the surrounding flavors under pressure.

If you don't want to use purchased beef stew meat, cut a 2½-pound boneless beef chuck roast or round into 2-inch pieces, discarding any large bits of fat, then freeze the chunks in a block in a sealed plastic bag.

1. Stir the liquid, flavor enhancer, onion, seasoning blend, and garlic (if using) in a **6-quart Instant Pot.** Set the chunk of frozen beef stew meat in the pot. (The block may sit up at an angle, leaning against the side of the insert.) Lock the lid onto the pot.

2.

Set the machine for	Set the level for	The valve must be	And set the time for	If necessary, press
PRESSURE COOK	MAX	—	35 minutes with the KEEP WARM setting off	START
MEAT/STEW, PRESSURE COOK, or MANUAL	HIGH	Closed	40 minutes with the KEEP WARM setting off	START

3. When the machine has finished cooking, turn it off and let its pressure **return to normal naturally,** about 35 minutes. Unlatch the lid and open the cooker. The meat will most likely have broken into chunks. If not, stirring it will break it apart. Stir in the vegetables and lock the lid back onto the pot.

4.

Set the machine for	Set the level for	The valve must be	And set the time for	If necessary, press
MEAT/STEW, PRESSURE COOK, or MANUAL	HIGH	Closed	3 minutes with the KEEP WARM setting off	START

5. Use the **quick-release method** to bring the pot's pressure back to normal. Unlatch the lid and open the cooker.

6.

Press the button for	Set it for	Set the time for	If necessary, press
SAUTÉ	MEDIUM, NORMAL, or CUSTOM 300°F	5 minutes	START

7. As the stew comes to a simmer, melt the butter in a microwave-safe dish in a microwave on high in 5-second increments, stirring occasionally. Once melted, use a fork or a whisk to mix the flour into the butter until dissolved (it won't quite be a paste). Stir this butter mixture into the simmering stew. Continue cooking, stirring all the while, until the stew has thickened somewhat, about 1 minute. Turn off the SAUTÉ function and set the pot aside for a couple of minutes to let the stew continue to thicken. Serve hot.

 Using a **-20°F CHEST FREEZER?** There is no difference in cooking times.

1 pound (4 to 5) cups frozen unseasoned chopped vegetables
Choose from any blend of frozen mixed vegetables (seasoning packets discarded), unseasoned hash brown cubes, cubed butternut squash, bell pepper strips, broccoli florets, green beans, cauliflower florets, or any combination of these (but do not use any leafy greens like spinach).

4 tablespoons (½ stick) unsalted butter

2 tablespoons all-purpose flour

Beyond

- For an **8-quart Instant Pot,** you must increase the liquid to 1½ cups.

- Beef stew is terrific over croutons. Large, unseasoned, plain ones are often sold in the bakery department of large supermarkets.

- It's even better over mashed potatoes (especially if you didn't put any potatoes in the vegetable mix). Rather than the standard butter-and-milk version of mashed potatoes, try making them with a little beef or chicken broth, some sour cream or softened cream cheese, a little Dijon mustard, a little table salt, and lots of ground black pepper.

Beef and Wheat Berry Stew

6 servings

2 cups beef or chicken broth

1 cup <u>frozen</u> chopped onion; or 1 medium yellow or white onion, peeled and chopped

1 tablespoon Worcestershire sauce

1 tablespoon minced and stemmed fresh rosemary leaves, or 2 teaspoons crumbled dried rosemary

2 teaspoons stemmed fresh thyme leaves, or 1 teaspoon dried thyme

1 teaspoon mild paprika

½ teaspoon table salt, optional

1 bay leaf

2 pounds <u>frozen</u> beef stew meat in 2-inch pieces

10 ounces (2 cups) "baby" carrots; or 4 medium carrots, peeled and cut into 1-inch pieces

1 cup raw wheat berries, preferably soft white wheat berries

This hearty stew features dried wheat berries, a whole grain that cooks beautifully in the Instant Pot. There are two varieties on the market: soft white (or "summer") wheat berries and hard red (or "winter") wheat berries. We suggest using the former because they cook a bit more quickly. They also have a milder, sweeter flavor.

If you can find only hard red wheat berries, you may need to add 5 minutes to either cooking time in step 4. Open the pot with the directed timing and release, then see if the harder wheat berries are soft yet. If not, lock the lid onto the pot and soldier on for another 5 minutes under pressure. The carrots will be much softer — which is not necessarily a bad thing but certainly a consideration.

See the headnote to the Beef and Vegetable Stew road map on page 126 for a way to cut up a boneless beef chuck roast and freeze it ahead of time for this recipe.

1. Stir the broth, onion, Worcestershire sauce, rosemary, thyme, paprika, salt (if using), and bay leaf in a **6- or 8-quart Instant Pot.** Set the block of frozen stew meat in this mixture. Lock the lid onto the pot.

2.

Set the machine for	Set the level for	The valve must be	And set the time for	If necessary, press
PRESSURE COOK	MAX	—	17 minutes with the KEEP WARM setting off	START
MEAT/STEW, PRESSURE COOK, or MANUAL	HIGH	Closed	20 minutes with the KEEP WARM setting off	START

3. Use the **quick-release method** to bring the pot's pressure back to normal. Unlatch the lid and open the cooker. Break the stew meat into individual pieces with the edge of a metal cooking spoon. Stir in the carrots and wheat berries, then lock the lid back onto the pot.

4.

Set the machine for	Set the level for	The valve must be	And set the time for	If necessary, press
PRESSURE COOK	MAX	—	35 minutes with the KEEP WARM setting off	START
MEAT/STEW, PRESSURE COOK, or MANUAL	HIGH	Closed	40 minutes with the KEEP WARM setting off	START

5. When the machine has finished cooking, turn it off and let its pressure **return to normal naturally,** about 35 minutes. Unlatch the lid and open the cooker. Remove the bay leaf and stir well before serving.

Beyond

- If you want to thicken the sauce, turn the SAUTÉ function to MEDIUM, NORMAL, or CUSTOM 300°F after you've opened the machine in step 5. Simmer for 2 minutes, stirring constantly, then stir in 1–2 tablespoons tomato paste. Simmer for about 1 minute, stirring constantly, until somewhat thickened. Turn off the SAUTÉ function and set the pot aside for a couple of minutes to continue to thicken up the stew.

- Or use the SAUTÉ function as above but stir in 1 ounce dried shiitake or porcini mushrooms, ground to a fine powder in a spice grinder.

✳ Using a **-20°F CHEST FREEZER?** There is no difference in cooking times.

Italian-Style Beef Stew

6 servings

One 14-ounce can diced
tomatoes packed in juice
(1⅔ cups)

½ cup red wine (of any sort) or
beef broth

½ cup **frozen** pearl onions or
frozen chopped onions; or
1 small yellow or white onion,
peeled and chopped

Up to ½ cup pitted black or
green olives

1½ teaspoons dried Italian
seasoning blend (a gluten-free
version, if that's a concern)

½ teaspoon red pepper flakes

2½ pounds **frozen** cubed beef
stew meat

One 14-ounce can artichoke
heart quarters packed in
water, drained (1½ cups)

¼ cup tomato paste

If you don't want to think through a road map for beef stew, here's a simple one that has the flavors of a pasta sauce but is more fully stocked with vegetables, making it a one-pot meal.

There's no salt because the olives give it plenty. In fact, we recommend using low-sodium tomatoes, tomato paste, and artichoke hearts to keep the dish from becoming too salty.

1. Mix the tomatoes, wine or broth, onions, olives, Italian seasoning blend, and red pepper flakes in a **6-quart Instant Pot.** Set the chunk of frozen beef cubes in the pot, submerging it as you can, although part of it may stick up and even lean against the insert. Lock the lid onto the pot.

2.

Set the machine for	Set the level for	The valve must be	And set the time for	If necessary, press
PRESSURE COOK	MAX	—	38 minutes with the KEEP WARM setting off	START
MEAT/STEW, PRESSURE COOK, or MANUAL	HIGH	Closed	44 minutes with the KEEP WARM setting off	START

3. When the machine has finished cooking, turn it off and let its pressure **return to normal naturally,** about 35 minutes. Unlatch the lid and open the cooker. If the stew meat has not broken apart, stir any clumps to get them in pieces.

4.

Press the button for	Set it for	Set the time for	If necessary, press
SAUTÉ	MEDIUM, NORMAL, or CUSTOM 300°F	10 minutes	START

5. Stir the stew until it comes to a full simmer. Stir in the artichoke heart quarters and tomato paste until the paste dissolves. Cook, stirring frequently, until somewhat thickened, 2–3 minutes. Turn off the SAUTÉ function and set the pot aside for a few minutes so the stew can continue to set up. Serve warm.

Beyond

- For an **8-quart Instant Pot,** you must increase the wine or broth to 1¼ cups and increase the stew meat to 3 pounds. The stew will then take up to 5 additional minutes to reduce to the right consistency in step 5.

- Although this is a one-pot meal and too "thin" to be considered a proper pasta sauce, you could indeed serve it over cooked and drained pasta, particularly spaghetti or even angel-hair pasta (or rice vermicelli, for that matter).

- Or serve it over cooked polenta.

- Or go all-American and ladle it over slices of cornbread (particularly split open and toasted cornbread).

 Using a **-20°F CHEST FREEZER?** There is no difference in cooking times.

All-American Pot Roast

6 servings

1½ cups beef broth

½ cup <u>frozen</u> chopped onion; or 1 small yellow or white onion, peeled and chopped

1 tablespoon Worcestershire sauce (or a gluten-free version, if that's a concern)

2 teaspoons peeled and minced garlic

One <u>frozen</u> 3- to 3½-pound boneless beef chuck roast

1 teaspoon mild paprika

1 teaspoon onion powder

1 teaspoon dried thyme

½ teaspoon ground black pepper

2 pounds peeled (and seeded as necessary) root vegetables, such as carrots, potatoes, turnips, sweet potatoes, rutabaga, butternut squash, and/or any winter squash, cut into 2-inch chunks

This recipe is like a road map because you can customize the root vegetables to whatever you prefer. The classics, of course, are carrots and potatoes; but there's no need to go with the same-old, same-old. Look around the supermarket for a selection of roots. Just remember the rule: The vegetables have to be in fairly large, 2-inch chunks so they cook evenly (and don't turn to mush). And remember that it's best to pair a "sweet" winter-keeping vegetable like butternut or winter squash with something a little more earthy or even bitter, like potatoes, turnips, or rutabaga.

We give the second cooking, the one after the root vegetables are added, only HIGH pressure (not MAX) to keep them a little less mushy. Note that these are *fresh*, not frozen, root vegetables. The fresh will yield a better flavor and texture with this timing.

We call for a lot of Worcestershire sauce in our recipes. It adds more flavor than salt, an umami richness that fills out a sauce better than some of the chemical "browning" enhancers on the store's shelves. If you want to go over the top, we've got an amazing recipe for homemade Worcestershire sauce on our website, bruceandmark.com. (Warning: It takes a few months to ripen in the fridge.)

1. Mix the broth, onion, Worcestershire sauce, and garlic in a **6- or 8-quart Instant Pot.** Set the pot's rack (with the handles up) or a large, open vegetable steamer inside the pot. Set the frozen chuck roast on the rack or in the steamer. Sprinkle the top of the meat evenly with the paprika, onion powder, thyme, and pepper. Lock the lid onto the pot.

2.

Set the machine for	Set the level for	The valve must be	And set the time for	If necessary, press
PRESSURE COOK	MAX	—	1 hour 20 minutes with the KEEP WARM setting off	START
MEAT/STEW, PRESSURE COOK, or MANUAL	HIGH	Closed	1 hour 30 minutes with the KEEP WARM setting off	START

3. Use the **quick-release method** to bring the pot's pressure back to normal. Unlatch the lid and open the cooker. Use kitchen tongs, silicone cooking mitts, or thick hot pads to remove the rack or steamer from the cooker, letting the chuck roast fall into the sauce below. Scatter the root vegetables over everything. Lock the lid back onto the pot.

4.

Set the machine for	Set the level for	The valve must be	And set the time for	If necessary, press
MEAT/STEW, PRESSURE COOK, or MANUAL	HIGH	Closed	10 minutes with the KEEP WARM setting off	START

5. When the machine has finished cooking, turn it off and let its pressure **return to normal naturally,** about 30 minutes. Unlatch the lid and open the cooker again. Using a large slotted spoon or large metal spatula and a meat fork, transfer the chuck roast to a nearby cutting board. Cool for a couple of minutes, then slice the meat into chunks to be served with the vegetables and sauce from the pot.

Beyond

- To thicken the sauce, remove the meat and the vegetables from the pot. Skim the sauce of any surface fat with a flatware spoon. Then bring the sauce to a simmer with the SAUTÉ function on HIGH, MORE, or CUSTOM 400°F. Whisk 1½ tablespoons cornstarch with 2 tablespoons water in a small bowl until uniform, then whisk this slurry into the simmering sauce. Cook, whisking all the while, until somewhat thickened, about 1 minute. Turn off the SAUTÉ function and serve the thickened sauce on the side.

- For a more complex stew, use a 50-50 combo of broth and either red wine or a dark beer.

- And for an even more complex stew, also add up to 1 tablespoon minced fresh sage leaves.

Using a **−20°F CHEST FREEZER?** Cook under pressure in step 2 for 1 hour 30 minutes on the MAX setting or for 1 hour 40 minutes on the HIGH setting. (There is no change to the cooking in step 4.)

Southwestern Pot Roast

6 servings

One 12-ounce bottle dark beer, preferably a plain porter or stout (no chocolate or coffee brews; gluten-free, if that's a concern)

5 ounces (1 cup) <u>frozen</u> pearl onions

1 canned chipotle in adobo sauce, stemmed, seeded, and minced

1 tablespoon adobo sauce from the can

1 tablespoon chili powder

2 teaspoons peeled and minced garlic

2 teaspoons ground cumin

½ teaspoon ground cinnamon

½ teaspoon table salt

One <u>frozen</u> 3- to 3½-pound boneless beef chuck roast

¼ cup ketchup

Two 15-ounce cans red kidney beans, drained and rinsed (3½ cups total)

This pot roast is a little fancy — even dinner-party worthy — given the big range of flavors (from the beer to the adobo sauce).

Note that the recipe calls for *one (canned) chipotle* in adobo sauce, not *one can* of chipotles in adobo sauce. What do you do with those remaining chiles and their sauce? They freeze really well. We often separate them into individual little containers with some sauce for each, a sure way to have one (and some sauce) on hand when we need it.

1. Stir the beer, pearl onions, chipotle, adobo sauce, chili powder, garlic, cumin, cinnamon, and salt in a **6- or 8-quart Instant Pot.** Set the pot's rack (with the handles up) or a large, open vegetable steamer inside the pot. Set the frozen chunk of chuck roast on the rack or in the steamer. Smear the ketchup on top of the beef, then lock the lid onto the pot.

2.

Set the machine for	Set the level for	The valve must be	And set the time for	If necessary, press
PRESSURE COOK	MAX	—	1 hour 20 minutes with the KEEP WARM setting off	START
MEAT/STEW, PRESSURE COOK, or MANUAL	HIGH	Closed	1 hour 30 minutes with the KEEP WARM setting off	START

3. Use the **quick-release method** to bring the pot's pressure back to normal. Unlatch the lid and open the cooker. Use kitchen tongs, silicone cooking mitts, or thick hot pads to remove the rack or the steamer, letting the roast fall into the liquid below. Scatter the beans over everything. Lock the lid back onto the pot.

4.

Set the machine for	Set the level for	The valve must be	And set the time for	If necessary, press
MEAT/STEW, PRESSURE COOK, or MANUAL	HIGH	Closed	10 minutes with the KEEP WARM setting off	START

5. When the machine has finished cooking, turn it off and let its pressure **return to normal naturally,** about 30 minutes. Unlatch the lid and open the cooker again. Use a large slotted spoon and a meat fork to transfer the chuck roast to a nearby cutting board. Cool the meat for a couple of minutes, then slice it into chunks to be served in bowls with the sauce and beans from the pot.

 Using a **-20°F CHEST FREEZER?** Cook under pressure in step 2 for 1 hour 30 minutes on the MAX setting or for 1 hour 40 minutes on the HIGH setting. (There is no change to the cooking in step 4.)

Beyond

- If you want to thicken the sauce, see the instructions in the *Beyond* of the All-American Pot Roast (page 133).

- If you want to add more vegetables, set a large, open vegetable steamer (perhaps the one you already used, if you didn't use the pot's rack) over everything (even the beans) in step 3 after the meat is back in the stew, then place up to 1 pound frozen butternut squash cubes in the steamer and cook as directed in step 4. The steamer will keep the cubes intact; they won't melt into the sauce as they would if set right into the sauce.

Mississippi-Style Short Ribs

6–8 servings

1 cup beef broth

One 16-ounce jar pepperoncini, drained

½ cup (1 stick) butter, cut into 4 pieces

½ cup **frozen** chopped onion; or 1 small yellow or white onion, peeled and chopped

¼ cup Worcestershire sauce (a gluten-free version, if that's a concern)

1 teaspoon dried sage

½ teaspoon ground allspice

½ teaspoon ground cinnamon

Eight **frozen** 8-ounce bone-in beef short ribs, each 3 to 4 inches long

Although Mississippi pot roast in the Instant Pot has become an internet sensation, we'd like to offer this buttery, salty, garlicky braise for frozen short ribs as a tastier version — without all that artificial and chemical junk found in packages of powdered dressing and gravy mixes. You might be surprised that this dish takes only 45 minutes once it comes to pressure. Because the short ribs are frozen and because they sit right in the sauce (cooling it down at first), the pot does take a long time to get up to pressure, as long as 30 minutes. But that's also cooking time, so the short ribs have a big head start before the pot ever reaches full pressure.

You'll see that the short ribs here are not those super-long ones sometimes sold at supermarkets. If those are all you can find, hand them to the butcher and ask him to cut them down to the right size. (And why are you paying so much for so much bone?)

1. Stir the broth, pepperoncini, butter, onion, Worcestershire sauce, sage, allspice, and cinnamon in a **6-quart Instant Pot.** Add the frozen short ribs in as much of one layer as possible (or with as little overlap as possible). Lock the lid onto the pot.

2.

Set the machine for	Set the level for	The valve must be	And set the time for	If necessary, press
PRESSURE COOK	MAX	—	40 minutes with the KEEP WARM setting off	START
MEAT/STEW, PRESSURE COOK, or MANUAL	HIGH	Closed	45 minutes with the KEEP WARM setting off	START

3. When the machine has finished cooking, turn it off and let it **return to natural pressure for 10 minutes.** Then use the **quick-release method** to get rid of any remaining pressure in the cooker. Unlatch the lid and open the pot. Serve the short ribs in bowls, with the sauce ladled around them.

 Using a **-20°F CHEST FREEZER?** There is no difference in cooking times.

Beyond

- For an **8-quart Instant Pot,** you must increase the broth to 1½ cups.

- The sauce is fatty (but flavorful). If it's too much for you, skim its surface with a flatware spoon before serving — or just let it sop into crusty bread or even mashed potatoes.

- For an even richer sauce, remove the beef and all vegetables, leaving the sauce in the pot. Bring that sauce to a simmer with the SAUTÉ function on HIGH, MORE, or CUSTOM 400°F. Cook, stirring occasionally, until reduced to half its original volume, 6–8 minutes. Then stir in up to ½ cup buttermilk until smooth and bring the sauce back to a boil. Boil for 2 minutes, then turn off the SAUTÉ function and remove the (hot!) insert from the pot.

Beef Bottom Round or Top Round with Beer and Carrots

6 servings

One 12-ounce bottle dark beer, preferably a plain porter or stout (no chocolate or coffee brews; gluten-free, if that's a concern)

½ cup frozen chopped onion; or 1 small yellow or white onion, peeled and chopped

1 tablespoon Dijon mustard

1 tablespoon Worcestershire sauce or a steak sauce like A.1. (gluten-free, if that's a concern)

1½ teaspoons mild paprika

1 teaspoon dried sage

½ teaspoon caraway seeds

½ teaspoon ground allspice

½ teaspoon table salt, optional (the mustard and Worcestershire sauce are salty)

½ teaspoon ground black pepper

One frozen 3½-pound beef top or bottom round roast

One 1-pound bag "baby" carrots

You can use either cut of beef for this braise, but the results will be quite different. Top round is a leaner cut, so the beef will ultimately be drier and the sauce less rich. Bottom round is fattier and so yields juicier bits in the bowls and a more satisfying sauce (if also more time on a cross-trainer).

Notice that this recipe calls for a bag of "baby" carrots, those small, cylindrical, already peeled carrots that make it into school lunches across the United States. If you'd rather use regular carrots, buy a 1-pound bag, peel the carrots, and slice them into 1½-inch sections.

1. Stir the beer, onion, mustard, Worcestershire or steak sauce, paprika, sage, caraway seeds, allspice, salt (if using), and pepper in a **6- or 8-quart Instant Pot.** Set the beef in the pot and lock on the lid.

2.

Set the machine for	Set the level for	The valve must be	And set the time for	If necessary, press
PRESSURE COOK	MAX	—	50 minutes with the KEEP WARM setting off	START
MEAT/STEW, PRESSURE COOK, or MANUAL	HIGH	Closed	1 hour with the KEEP WARM setting off	START

3. Use the **quick-release method** to bring the pot's pressure back to normal. Unlatch the lid and open the cooker. Use a meat fork to turn the beef over. Add the carrots, then lock the lid back onto the pot.

4.

Set the machine for	Set the level for	The valve must be	And set the time for	If necessary, press
PRESSURE COOK	MAX	—	20 minutes with the KEEP WARM setting off	START
MEAT/STEW, PRESSURE COOK, or MANUAL	HIGH	Closed	17 minutes with the KEEP WARM setting off	START

5. Again, use the **quick-release method** to bring the pot's pressure back to normal. Unlatch the lid and open the pot again. Use a slotted spoon and a meat fork to transfer the beef to a nearby cutting board. Let it rest for a couple of minutes, then carve it into chunks to be served in bowls with the carrots and sauce from the cooker.

 Using a **-20°F CHEST FREEZER?** Cook under pressure in step 2 for 1 hour 5 minutes on the MAX setting or for 1 hour 15 minutes on the HIGH setting.

Beyond

- We offer up a two-step process, but the best results are actually attained with three steps: Cook the beef for 25 minutes at MAX or 30 minutes at HIGH, then do a **quick release,** open the pot, and flip the meat over. Have another go at 25 minutes at MAX or 30 minutes at HIGH followed by a second **quick release.** Add the carrots and carry on with step 4 (with more cooking and releasing). But a three-step cooking process may be too much effort for some nights.

- To thicken the sauce, remove the meat and vegetables from the pot. Melt 4 tablespoons (½ stick) butter in a microwave on high in 10-second increments, then stir in 3 tablespoons all-purpose flour until smooth. Bring the sauce in the pot to a simmer, using the SAUTÉ function on HIGH, MORE, or CUSTOM 400°F. Stir this butter mixture into the simmering sauce until somewhat thickened, about 1 minute. Turn off the SAUTÉ function before ladling the sauce over the servings in bowls.

Beef Bottom Round or Top Round with Horseradish and Parsnips

6 servings

1 cup beef broth

1 tablespoon distilled white vinegar

Up to 2 fresh tarragon sprigs or 3 fresh thyme sprigs

1 bay leaf

One frozen 3½-pound beef top or bottom round roast

⅓ cup jarred prepared white horseradish

6 medium parsnips, peeled but left whole

In a book of simple recipes for pantry cooking, here's our biggest flight of fancy. The horseradish actually mellows as it cooks, turning sweet and irresistible with those earthy parsnips. If you find the parsnips won't lie flat in the pot, cut off the thinner ends so they will (these cut-off bits can be dropped into the sauce). The whole dish is super aromatic and meaty, a wonderful bit of newfangled comfort food for a Sunday supper.

Although the previous recipe for bottom or top round roast had a *Beyond* suggestion for thickening the sauce, we prefer this sauce thinner. It's sweet, aromatic, and herbaceous, almost like a rich soup poured over the beef and parsnips.

1. Stir the broth, vinegar, tarragon or thyme, and bay leaf in a **6-quart Instant Pot.** Set the meat in the pot, then lock on the lid.

2.

Set the machine for	Set the level for	The valve must be	And set the time for	If necessary, press
PRESSURE COOK	MAX	—	50 minutes with the KEEP WARM setting off	START
MEAT/STEW, PRESSURE COOK, or MANUAL	HIGH	Closed	1 hour with the KEEP WARM setting off	START

3. Use the **quick-release method** to bring the pot's pressure back to normal. Unlatch the lid and open the cooker. Turn the meat over in the sauce and smear the horseradish over the top. Set the parsnips in the pot and lock the lid back on.

4.

Set the machine for	Set the level for	The valve must be	And set the time for	If necessary, press
PRESSURE COOK	MAX	—	10 minutes with the KEEP WARM setting off	START
MEAT/STEW, PRESSURE COOK, or MANUAL	HIGH	Closed	12 minutes with the KEEP WARM setting off	START

5. When the machine has finished cooking, turn it off and let its pressure **return to normal naturally,** about 30 minutes. Unlatch the lid and open the cooker again. Fish out and remove the herb sprigs and bay leaf. Use a big slotted spoon and a meat fork to transfer the roast to a nearby cutting board. Let it rest for a couple of minutes, then carve it into chunks to be served in bowls with the parsnips and sauce from the cooker.

 Using a **-20°F CHEST FREEZER?** Cook under pressure in step 2 for 1 hour 5 minutes on the MAX setting or for 1 hour 15 minutes on the HIGH setting.

Beyond

- For an **8-quart Instant Pot,** you must use 1½ cups beef broth.

- For an additional step that helps the meat bathe more evenly in the sauce, see the three-step cooking suggestion for the previous bottom or top round recipe (page 139).

- Make your own croutons to scatter over the stew: Cut a baguette into ½-inch-thick rounds and arrange in a single layer on a large, lipped baking sheet. Drizzle the bread evenly with olive oil, then bake in a 350°F oven for 10 minutes without turning.

- Better yet, make pumpernickel croutons.

Pulled Flank Steak

4–6 servings

One 28-ounce can whole tomatoes packed in juice (3½ cups)

2 tablespoons dark brown sugar

2 tablespoons apple cider vinegar

2 tablespoons mild smoked paprika

1 tablespoon Dijon or prepared yellow mustard

1 tablespoon Worcestershire sauce (a gluten-free version, if that's a concern)

1 teaspoon ground coriander

½ teaspoon ground cloves

One <u>frozen</u> 2-pound beef flank steak

Here's our recipe for pulled beef. While the Instant Pot makes excellent pulled beef brisket and other cuts (see our recipes in *The Instant Pot Bible*), they don't fare as well from their frozen state. They take so long to thaw and cook that they become unduly soft, even squishy. But we found that flank steak has just the right amount of fat within its fibers that run in one direction, all the better for pulling.

A flank steak is usually sold folded up, even if it's frozen — and only a steak folded in this way will fit in the pot. If you buy a fresh flank steak and freeze it to make this dish later on, remove the meat from its packaging and fold it in half or thirds before freezing it in a sealed plastic bag.

1. Pour the tomatoes and their juice into a **6-quart Instant Pot.** Clean and dry your hands, then crush the whole tomatoes to bits in the pot. (Or use a pastry cutter to mush them up in the pot.) Stir in the brown sugar, vinegar, smoked paprika, mustard, Worcestershire sauce, coriander, and cloves until the brown sugar dissolves. Set the frozen flank steak in the pot and lock on the lid.

2.

Set the machine for	Set the level for	The valve must be	And set the time for	If necessary, press
PRESSURE COOK	MAX	—	1 hour 10 minutes with the KEEP WARM setting off	START
MEAT/STEW, PRESSURE COOK, or MANUAL	HIGH	Closed	1 hour 20 minutes with the KEEP WARM setting off	START

3. When the machine has finished cooking, turn it off and let its pressure **return to normal naturally,** about 30 minutes. Unlatch the lid and open the cooker. Cool for a couple of minutes, then shred the meat with two forks, pulling with its grain the length of the cut as if you're combing hair or maybe carding wool. Stir these shreds into the sauce in the pot and set aside for 5 minutes, with the lid askew over the pot, so the meat can absorb some more of the sauce. Serve warm.

Beyond

- For an **8-quart Instant Pot,** you must add ½ cup beef broth or red wine with the tomatoes.

- Serve the pulled beef with or without buns or tortillas but certainly garnished with sour cream, avocado slices, grated cheese, and/or pickled jalapeño rings.

- The pulled beef isn't spicy at all. Either pass a hot sauce at the table or add up to 1 tablespoon red pepper flakes with the other spices in step 1.

- Use the pulled beef as a filling for enchiladas: Wrap it in corn tortillas, lay these seam-side down in a baking dish, and top with enchilada sauce or salsa, all covered with shredded cheese. Bake covered in a 350°F oven for 10 minutes, then uncovered until bubbling and gooey.

 Using a **-20°F CHEST FREEZER?** There is no difference in cooking times.

5

Pork

Pork is luxurious enough (that is, fatty enough) to stand up to the pot's pressure without any problems. That's why it may be the single best *frozen* ingredient to cook in an Instant Pot—so we've got lots of ideas for pork chops, loin, shoulder, sausages, and even ham.

You might be surprised to discover no recipes for pork tenderloin. It's not that it *couldn't* work. It's that the frozen cut won't fit in a 6-quart Instant Pot—and often not even in an 8-quart pot. Back in the day, pork tenderloins were small, maybe 1 pound each. Now they're monster-sized. In their frozen-hard state, you'd have to stand them up in the pot and you wouldn't be able to get the lid on properly. Even if you find a smaller tenderloin, part of it would sit in the hot liquid while the rest would stay up near the top of the pot, resulting in one burned and one raw end.

That said, there are recipes for pork *loin*—mostly because a loin is about double the diameter of a tenderloin. We call for a specific size of pork loin (3 pounds), which is about the same as putting a fat roast in the pot.

We worked out our timings to hit the USDA pork guideline: 145°F internal temperature. In other words, the pork may still be a bit pink at its center. It'll be juicier, too, and more flavorful. Don't overcook pork. It's perfectly safe at 145°F. Use an instant-read meat thermometer to be sure.

You're probably least likely to find cuts of pork already frozen at the store. So you have an opportunity to do a little prep, if you want. Take the pork out of its packaging, remove and discard the diaper, then freeze the meat in a sealed storage bag. You'll have a much easier time making any of these recipes if you don't have to remove the diaper from a frozen piece of pork. And making it easy is what this book is all about!

Road Map: **Barbecue Pork Loin**

6 servings

1½ cups purchased barbecue sauce of any sort

This one is *not* pulled pork. Rather, the pork loin is sliced into rounds and served with the barbecue sauce.

Remember that the liquid you choose will dramatically affect the sweetness of the finished dish. If you go with beer or cider, you'll want to use a far less-sweet barbecue sauce, probably a hot one with chipotles in the mix.

1 cup thin liquid

Choose from water, broth of any sort, beer of any sort (gluten-free, if that is a concern), or unsweetened apple cider.

1. Stir the barbecue sauce and liquid in a **6- to 8-quart Instant Pot.** Set the pork loin fat-side down in the pot and turn it to coat it in the sauce, leaving it fat-side up. Lock the lid onto the cooker.

One <u>frozen</u> 3-pound boneless center-cut pork loin

2.

Set the machine for	Set the level for	The valve must be	And set the time for	If necessary, press
PRESSURE COOK	MAX	—	45 minutes with the KEEP WARM setting off	START
MEAT/STEW, PRESSURE COOK, or MANUAL	HIGH	Closed	50 minutes with the KEEP WARM setting off	START

3. When the machine has finished cooking, turn it off and let its pressure **return to normal naturally,** about 45 minutes. Unlatch the lid and open the cooker. Insert an instant-read meat thermometer into the center of the pork loin and check that the meat registers 145°F. If not, lock the lid back onto the cooker and cook for another 10 minutes at HIGH pressure, followed by a **quick release.** Transfer the pork loin to a nearby cutting board. Set aside for 10 minutes.

4.

Press the button for	Set it for	Set the time for	If necessary, press
SAUTÉ	MEDIUM, NORMAL, or CUSTOM 300°F	20 minutes	START

5. Bring the sauce in the cooker to a simmer, stirring occasionally. Cook, stirring once in a while, until reduced to the consistency of a thick barbecue sauce, about 12 minutes. Turn off the SAUTÉ function. Slice the pork loin into ½-inch-thick rounds and serve with the sauce ladled on top.

 Using a **-20°F CHEST FREEZER?** Cook under pressure in step 2 for 55 minutes on the MAX setting or for 1 hour on the HIGH setting.

Beyond

- Since this dish isn't pulled, it's best over a bed of vegetables or grains. Try steamed or sautéed spinach or kale. Or serve it over a cooked whole grain like wheat berries mixed with herbs and/or diced carrots. Or go all out with a wild rice pilaf.

- This is probably the best pork dish in this book for sandwiches. Slice the pork loin into ¼-inch-thick rounds, then store in the reduced sauce in a sealed container in the fridge for up to 3 days. Lift them out of the sauce and serve them on kaiser rolls with purchased coleslaw or thinly sliced red onions and lots of pickle relish.

Pulled Pork

6 servings

One 12-ounce bottle dark beer, such as a stout, brown ale, or porter (preferably either a plain bottling or a coffee stout or porter; gluten-free, if that is a concern); or cola, Dr Pepper, or root beer

One <u>frozen</u> 3½-pound boneless pork shoulder or butt

⅓ cup dried barbecue rub blend or Southwestern seasoning mix

We'll admit we first got into pressure cooking because of the promise of pulled pork in less time than it takes to tend a smoker. There are no burned ends or crunchy bits, but the meat is tender and juicy, the best for sandwiches. (Leftovers are terrific for a weekend breakfast when topped with fried eggs!)

But it bears stating that this recipe takes a long time — the meat has to thaw, then cook until tender. It will throw off a great deal of liquid. The pot may be swamped when you open it. But when you boil the liquid down, it will be the perfect sauce for the shreds of meat.

If you use cola for the liquid, it's best if it's not a diet soda. Yes, diet soda will work. But the overall feel of the sauce, its thickness and texture, will be compromised by the lack of sugar.

1. Pour the beer or cola into a **6- or 8-quart Instant Pot.** Set the pot's rack in the pot with the handles up. (The rack is better than a vegetable steamer here because the rack is a little lower than a steamer and the meat will be bathed in the released liquid more quickly.) Set the frozen hunk of pork on the rack. Sprinkle the spice mixture over the meat. Lock the lid onto the pot.

2.

Set the machine for	Set the level for	The valve must be	And set the time for	If necessary, press
PRESSURE COOK	MAX	——	2 hours with the KEEP WARM setting off	START
MEAT/STEW, PRESSURE COOK, or MANUAL	HIGH	Closed	2 hours 10 minutes with the KEEP WARM setting off	START

3. When the machine has finished cooking, turn it off and let its pressure **return to normal naturally,** about 45 minutes.

4. Unlatch the lid and open the cooker. Use a large metal spatula and a meat fork to transfer the meat to a nearby cutting board. (It can be tough to get it out of the pot. If you're short, consider *unplugging* the cooker and setting the whole thing, once opened, in a dry sink. You now won't need to reach up and into the machine to get the meat out. Put the cutting board right at the sink's edge.) Use a cooking spoon to skim off and discard the fat on top of the liquid in the pot.

5.

Press the button for	Set it for	Set the time for	If necessary, press
SAUTÉ	HIGH, MORE, or CUSTOM 400°F	15 minutes	START

6. Bring the sauce in the cooker to a boil, stirring occasionally. Meanwhile, chop the pork into small bits, discarding any blobs of fat or cartilage in the mix.

7. Continue boiling the liquid in the pot, stirring occasionally, until reduced to half its original amount, about 10 minutes. Turn off the SAUTÉ function and stir the chopped and shredded meat into the sauce. Set aside for 5 minutes so the meat continues to absorb sauce.

 Using a **-20°F CHEST FREEZER?** Cook under pressure for 2 hours 10 minutes on the MAX setting or for 2½ hours on the HIGH setting.

Beyond

- If you want to make your own rub for the pork, nix the seasoning blend and stir together 1 tablespoon dark brown sugar, 1 tablespoon mild smoked paprika, 2 teaspoons ground black pepper, 2 teaspoons onion powder, 2 teaspoons table salt, 1 teaspoon ground dried mustard, 1 teaspoon garlic powder, 1 teaspoon dried oregano, and 1 teaspoon ground cumin.

- Pulled pork calls out for garnishes of pickle relish, pickled jalapeño rings, maybe sour cream, maybe deli mustard, and certainly either pickled or thinly sliced onions. Buns are optional.

- Once cooled, make quesadillas with the pulled pork. Place some meat without a lot of juice on a flour tortilla with shredded cheese and perhaps some pickled jalapeño rings. Top with a second tortilla, then brown in a nonstick skillet set over medium heat, turning once, until crisp, about 6 minutes.

Curried Pork Loin and Potatoes

6 servings

One 12-ounce can ginger ale

1½ tablespoons yellow curry powder

½ teaspoon ground cinnamon

½ teaspoon table salt

One frozen 3-pound boneless center-cut pork loin

1½ pounds small yellow potatoes, halved

Ginger ale gives the right amount of sweetness (and a gingery flavor) to this easy dinner. Yes, you can use a sugar-free ginger ale. But as with the Pulled Pork (pages 148–149), the sauce will seem thinner, even if you go to the trouble of thickening it, because of the lack of sugar. The compromise may (or may not) be worth it.

It's important that the pork loin sits in the pot with the fat side up. Otherwise, the fat will burn against the bottom of the pot before the meat has a chance to thaw and start cooking.

1. Mix the ginger ale, curry powder, cinnamon, and salt in a **6- or 8-quart Instant Pot.** Set the pork loin in the liquid, fat side up. Lock the lid onto the pot.

2.

Set the machine for	Set the level for	The valve must be	And set the time for	If necessary, press
PRESSURE COOK	MAX	——	25 minutes with the KEEP WARM setting off	START
MEAT/STEW, PRESSURE COOK, or MANUAL	HIGH	Closed	30 minutes with the KEEP WARM setting off	START

3. When the machine has finished cooking, turn it off and let its pressure **return to normal naturally,** about 40 minutes. Unlatch the lid and open the cooker. Scatter the potatoes around the meat. Lock the lid back onto the pot.

4.

Set the machine for	Set the level for	The valve must be	And set the time for	If necessary, press
PRESSURE COOK	MAX	—	12 minutes with the KEEP WARM setting off	START
MEAT/STEW, PRESSURE COOK, or MANUAL	HIGH	Closed	15 minutes with the KEEP WARM setting off	START

5. Use the **quick-release method** to bring the pot's pressure back to normal. Unlatch the lid and open the cooker. Insert an instant-read meat thermometer into the center of the pork loin and check that the meat registers 145°F. If not, remove the potatoes from the pot, lock the lid back on, and cook for another 10 minutes at HIGH pressure, followed by a **quick release.**

6. Transfer the pork loin to a nearby cutting board and cool for 5 minutes. Slice into ½-inch-thick rounds; serve with the potatoes and some of the sauce from the pot.

 Using a **–20°F CHEST FREEZER?** Cook under pressure for 35 minutes on the MAX setting or for 40 minutes on the HIGH setting in step 2 before adding the potatoes.

Beyond

- For a heavier ginger flavor, substitute ginger beer for the ginger ale.

- Gussy up the dish by using a red or yellow curry paste, rather than curry powder. If so, omit the cinnamon and salt. Instead, add one 4-inch cinnamon stick to the pot with the ginger ale.

- Or make your own dried curry powder blend by mixing together 1½ teaspoons ground coriander, 1½ teaspoons ground dried turmeric, ½ teaspoon ground cumin, ½ teaspoon dried thyme, ¼ teaspoon grated nutmeg, and ¼ teaspoon ground cloves.

- To enrich the sauce, remove the pork from the pot and use a slotted spoon to transfer the potatoes to a serving dish. Bring the sauce in the pot to a simmer, using the SAUTÉ function on MEDIUM, NORMAL, or CUSTOM 300°F. Whisk in ½ cup coconut milk and simmer, stirring often, for 2–3 minutes to lose the raw taste of the coconut milk. Turn off the SAUTÉ function and spoon the sauce over the potatoes and slices of pork in serving bowls.

Italian-Style Braised Pork Chops

4 servings

1 cup chicken broth

2 tablespoons balsamic vinegar

2 teaspoons stemmed thyme leaves, or 1 teaspoon dried thyme

¼ teaspoon grated fresh nutmeg, or ⅛ teaspoon ground nutmeg

¼ teaspoon red pepper flakes

¼ teaspoon table salt

One 16-ounce bag **frozen** bell pepper strips (4 cups)

Four **frozen** 6- to 8-ounce center-cut boneless pork loin chops

This simple braise packs a lot of flavor into each bite, partly because of the way the chops thaw and release their flavor into the sauce. Note the unusual method of setting the chops in the sauce: standing up and leaning against each other, with space between their bottom edges. If you stack them up like bricks, the bottom chop can burn against the hot pot (it will cool the liquid down too far before it thaws and starts to cook) while the one on top can end up undercooked, even raw.

Because of the way the bell pepper strips cook in the sauce, we do not recommend using fresh bell pepper for this recipe.

1. Stir the broth, vinegar, thyme, nutmeg, red pepper flakes, and salt in a **6-quart Instant Pot.** Mix in the frozen pepper strips, then set the pork chops in the pot so they stand up on their sides and lean against each other and the side of the insert with room between each for liquid and pepper strips (in other words, not in a stack). Lock the lid onto the pot.

Beyond

- For an **8-quart Instant Pot,** you must increase all the ingredients by 50 percent.

- Drizzle the servings with extra-virgin olive oil and even a little more balsamic vinegar, particularly a syrupy aged balsamic.

- Add more pop to the sauce by stirring up to 1 teaspoon finely grated lemon zest and/or 1 bay leaf into the mixture with the pepper strips.

- Serve the pork chops on opened baked potatoes with the sauce ladled on top. Garnish each serving with a pat of butter.

2.

Set the machine for	Set the level for	The valve must be	And set the time for	If necessary, press
PRESSURE COOK	MAX	——	16 minutes with the KEEP WARM setting off	START
MEAT/ STEW, PRESSURE COOK, or MANUAL	HIGH	Closed	20 minutes with the KEEP WARM setting off	START

3. Use the **quick-release method** to bring the pot's pressure back to normal. Unlatch the lid and open the cooker. Transfer the pork chops to serving plates and spoon some of the sauce and peppers over each.

 Using a **-20°F CHEST FREEZER?**
There is no difference in cooking times.

Chicken Noodle
Soup (page 24)

Butternut Squash Bisque (page 26) with a grilled cheese sandwich

Tortilla Soup (page 34)

Tater Tot Soup
(page 36)
garnished with
minced chives
and crunchy
Tater Tots

Chinese Dumpling Soup (page 40) with a little *sambal oelek* on the side

Road Map: Ravioli (page 48), tossed
with pesto and red pepper flakes

Mac and Cheese and Meatballs (page 54)

Ground Beef and Noodle Goulash (page 56) with coarsely ground red pepper on the side

Ziti with Sausage and Peppers
(page 64)

Easy Scallops
Alfredo
(page 70),
garnished
with peas and
ground black
pepper

Road Map:
Bone-In Chicken
Breasts (page 76)
with an arugula
salad on the side

Chicken Fajitas (page 82) with all the fixings

**Chicken Teriyaki
(page 84) with
sticky short-grain
white rice on the side**

Buffalo Chicken Wings (page 90) with celery sticks and blue cheese dip

**Turkey Tacos (page 96),
garnished with cheese, lettuce,
and pickled jalapeño rings**

Chinatown-Style Chop Suey with Ground Turkey (page 102) over crunchy chow mein noodles

Turkey Meatballs with
Buttery Rice Pilaf (page 104)

Road Map: Burgers (page 110) with lettuce, tomato, and mayo

Road Map: Pot Pie (page 112)

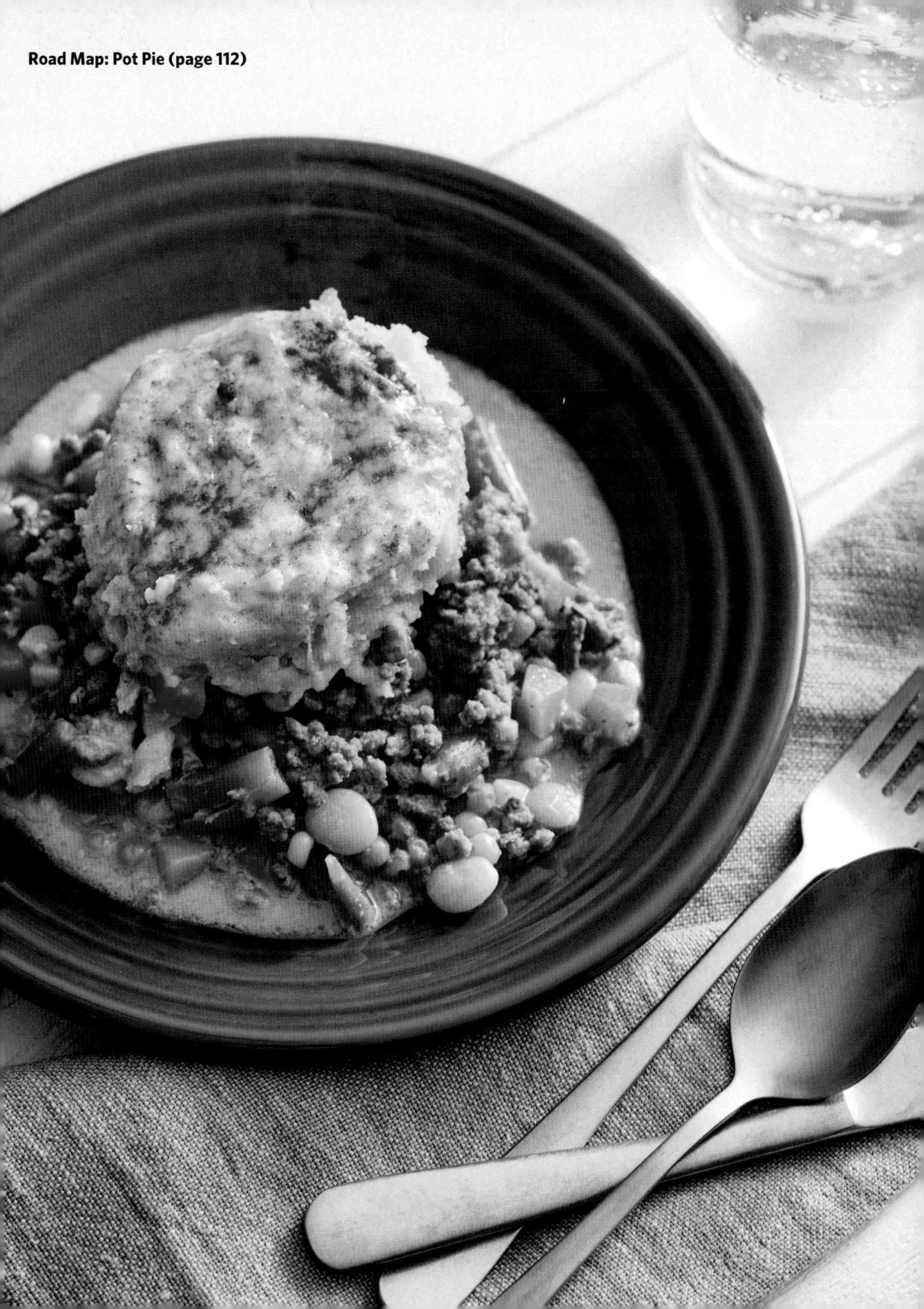

French Dip Sandwiches
(page 115)

**Meatball Chili
(page 120), garnished
with cheese and minced
fresh jalapeño chile**

The raw ingredients for All-American Pot Roast

All-American Pot Roast with potatoes
(page 132)

**Mississippi-Style Short Ribs
(page 136)**

Pulled Flank Steak (page 142), served in flour tortillas with minced fresh jalapeño chile and cilantro

Italian-Style Braised Pork Chops
(page 146), served in an opened baked potato

Road Map: Barbecue Pork Loin (page 152), served as a sandwich with red onion and pickle relish

The raw ingredients for Mongolian-Style Pork Stew

Mongolian-Style Pork Stew
(page 154)

Cheesy Ham and Potato
Casserole (page 156)

Sweet and Sour Shrimp (page 166) on a bed of wilted kale

Shrimp Scampi (page 170) over angel-hair pasta

Simple Steamed Salmon Fillets (page 171) served over a kale Caesar salad

**Cod Fillets with Tomatoes and Zucchini
(page 174), served with garlic toast**

Butter-Poached Mahi-Mahi (page 176), over steamed asparagus

Braised Pork Chops with Sweet Potatoes

4 servings

Because these pork chops sit up on top of the sweet potato wedges, they don't need to stand on their sides in any special way (as in the previous boneless chop recipe). In essence, the chops sit up out of the liquid as they pressure-steam in the pot.

And the type of pressure release is different here than in the previous recipe because of the sweet potatoes. They actually take a little longer to cook than the chops. If we left them at high pressure for long enough to get tender, the chops would be tough. But by using a modified natural release, the sweet potatoes can get tender (in those 10 minutes without full pressure) while the chops stay juicier.

1 cup unsweetened apple juice or cider

½ teaspoon ground cinnamon

½ teaspoon granulated white sugar

½ teaspoon table salt

Two 10-ounce sweet potatoes, peeled and each cut lengthwise into 4 quarters

Four <u>frozen</u> 6- to 8-ounce boneless center-cut pork loin chops

4 tablespoons (½ stick) unsalted butter, cut into 3 or 4 pieces

2 teaspoons dried-herb poultry seasoning blend

1. Stir the cider, cinnamon, sugar, and salt in a **6-quart Instant Pot.** Set the sweet potatoes in the cooker. Overlap the frozen pork chops on top of them, sort of like shingles. Put the butter on top of the chops, then sprinkle it all with the dried seasoning. Lock the lid onto the cooker.

2.

Set the machine for	Set the level for	The valve must be	And set the time for	If necessary, press
PRESSURE COOK	MAX	—	16 minutes with the KEEP WARM setting off	START
MEAT/STEW, PRESSURE COOK, or MANUAL	HIGH	Closed	20 minutes with the KEEP WARM setting off	START

3. When the machine has finished cooking, turn it off and let its pressure **return to normal naturally** for 10 minutes. Then use the **quick-release method** to get rid of any residual pressure in the pot. Unlatch the lid and open the cooker. Transfer the pork chops, sweet potato wedges, and sauce to serving bowls.

 Using a **−20°F CHEST FREEZER?**
There is no difference in cooking times.

Beyond

- For an **8-quart Instant Pot,** you must increase all the ingredients by 50 percent.

- Because you don't need to stack these chops on their sides, you can substitute four <u>frozen</u>, 8-ounce, bone-in, ½-inch-thick, pork loin chops for the boneless ones.

- If you don't want to use a bottled poultry seasoning blend, substitute 1 teaspoon dried sage, ½ teaspoon dried thyme, ¼ teaspoon dried marjoram, and ¼ teaspoon grated nutmeg.

Mongolian-Style Pork Stew

4 servings

¾ cup unsweetened apple juice
or cider

¼ cup regular or reduced-
sodium soy sauce or tamari

1½ tablespoons honey

1 tablespoon peeled and minced
fresh ginger, or 1 teaspoon
ground dried ginger

One <u>frozen</u> 2½-pound cut-up
bone-in pork shoulder

1 pound (4 to 5 cups) <u>frozen</u>
unseasoned mixed
vegetables, preferably an
Asian-style blend (any
seasoning packet discarded)

2 tablespoons water, optional

1½ tablespoons cornstarch,
optional

Here's our porky version of the *beef* stew that's been making the rounds on social media. (It's sometimes called a "stir-fry" online, but we can't understand how it's anything but a braise — nor even what truly makes it "Mongolian.") We think our version is better because 1) it uses pork (which is a sweeter meat), and 2) the bone adds a great deal of flavor to the sauce for a more satisfying meal.

Notice that this recipe calls for cut-up bone-in pork shoulder. It's easy to find in the South; it's a bit more difficult to track down elsewhere. If you can't, select a fresh pork shoulder and have the butcher cut it into 1½- to 2-inch chunks before freezing these in a sealed plastic bag. Or substitute bone-in country-style pork ribs, cut into 2-inch pieces and frozen in a bag. Or use regular pork stew meat (although you'll then miss out on the flavor of that bony goodness in the sauce).

Steps 6 and 7 ask you to thicken the sauce with cornstarch. In truth, you needn't. You can skip those steps and just serve the much "looser" sauce with the pork.

1. Stir the juice or cider, soy sauce or tamari, honey, and ginger in a **6-quart Instant Pot.** Set the block of frozen pork meat in the liquids (it may rest against the side of the pot's insert). Lock the lid onto the pot.

2.

Set the machine for	Set the level for	The valve must be	And set the time for	If necessary, press
PRESSURE COOK	MAX	—	35 minutes with the KEEP WARM setting off	START
MEAT/STEW, PRESSURE COOK, or MANUAL	HIGH	Closed	40 minutes with the KEEP WARM setting off	START

3. Use the **quick-release method** to bring the pot's pressure back to normal. Unlatch the lid and open the cooker. Stir the pork until it breaks into chunks (it may have already), then stir in the vegetables. Lock the lid back onto the pot.

4.

Set the machine for	Set the level for	The valve must be	And set the time for	If necessary, press
MEAT/STEW, PRESSURE COOK, or MANUAL	HIGH	Closed	1 minute with the KEEP WARM setting off	START

5. Use the **quick-release method** to bring the pot's pressure back to normal. Again, unlatch the lid and open the cooker.

6.

Press the button for	Set it for	Set the time for	If necessary, press
SAUTÉ	MEDIUM, NORMAL, or CUSTOM 300°F	5 minutes	START

7. If you like, bring the liquid in the pot to a simmer, stirring occasionally. Meanwhile, whisk the water and cornstarch in a small bowl or teacup until smooth. When the liquid is simmering in the pot, stir in this slurry and continue cooking, stirring constantly, until the sauce has thickened somewhat, about 1 minute. Turn off the SAUTÉ function and set the pot aside for a couple of minutes so that the sauce continues to set up.

 Using a **–20°F CHEST FREEZER?** There is no difference in cooking times.

Beyond

- For an **8-quart Instant Pot,** you must increase the cider or juice to 1¼ cups and increase the bone-in pork shoulder to 3 pounds.

- Serve the stew over cooked rice, white or brown. We prefer a medium-grain rice, like Arborio (again, either white or brown).

- Or try it over cooked and drained rice noodles.

- Garnish the servings with minced scallions or chives, cilantro leaves, and/or chopped, salted peanuts.

Cheesy Ham and Potato Casserole

4 servings

1 cup chicken or beef broth

2 pounds frozen unseasoned
hash brown cubes

Two frozen 8-ounce thin
boneless ham steaks

1½ teaspoons stemmed and
minced sage leaves, or
½ teaspoon dried sage

1 teaspoon stemmed thyme
leaves, or ½ teaspoon dried
thyme

1 teaspoon onion powder

¼ teaspoon cayenne, optional

8 ounces (2 cups) shredded
Swiss or Cheddar cheese

This recipe is sort of like a hash converted into a dinner casserole. The frozen, boneless ham steaks are fairly easy to break into pieces. However, if you can't get them into pieces, just lay them on top of the potato cubes in the pot.

Some cured meats (like the ham here) can contain glutens in their preservatives and can be subject to cross-contamination at processing facilities, particularly if they've been processed at a facility that also makes sausages with a wheat additive or filler. Use only certified gluten-free ham, if that is a concern.

1.

Press the button for	Set it for	Set the time for	If necessary, press
SAUTÉ	MEDIUM, NORMAL, or CUSTOM 300°F	5 minutes	START

2. Pour the broth into a **6-quart Instant Pot** and heat it until wisps of steam rise off the liquid. (It can even come to a very low simmer — but not too much because you'll lose the liquid necessary for the pressure.)

3. Make an even layer of half the hash brown cubes in the pot. Turn off the SAUTÉ function. Break the ham steaks into thirds and set them on top of the potatoes. Make an even layer of the remaining potato cubes on the ham. Sprinkle the sage, thyme, onion powder, and cayenne (if using) evenly over the potatoes. Lock the lid onto the pot.

4.

Set the machine for	Set the level for	The valve must be	And set the time for	If necessary, press
PRESSURE COOK	MAX	—	3 minutes with the KEEP WARM setting off	START
MEAT/STEW, PRESSURE COOK, or MANUAL	HIGH	Closed	4 minutes with the KEEP WARM setting off	START

5. Use the **quick-release method** to bring the pot's pressure back to normal. Unlatch the lid and open the cooker. Sprinkle the cheese evenly over the top of the dish. Set the lid askew over the pot and set aside for 5 minutes to let the cheese melt before serving by the big spoonful.

Using a **-20°F CHEST FREEZER?** There is no difference in cooking times.

Beyond

- For an **8-quart Instant Pot,** you must increase all the ingredients by 50 percent.

- The casserole is a great breakfast, too! Top each serving with a poached egg.

- While we like this one when it's straightforward with Swiss or Cheddar on top, you can use any shredded cheese — or a blend — that you like.

- If you want more heat in the dish, pass hot red pepper sauce at the table.

Buttery Cajun Rice with Smoked Sausage

4 servings

3 cups chicken broth

1½ cups raw white basmati rice
(see page 9)

1 cup <u>frozen</u> chopped onion; or
1 medium yellow or white
onion, peeled and chopped

2 ounces (½ cup) <u>frozen</u> bell
pepper strips; or 1 small
green or red bell pepper,
stemmed, cored, and cut into
thin strips

1 tablespoon Cajun seasoning
blend

½ teaspoon salt, optional (check
to see if the seasoning blend
includes salt)

4 tablespoons (½ stick) unsalted
butter, cut into small chunks

1½ pounds <u>frozen</u> smoked
kielbasa links (gluten-free, if
that is a concern)

In this quick casserole, the sausage pressure-steams over the rice as it cooks. The sausages cannot be dropped directly into the rice or they'll cool the liquid too much and the rice will stick to the bottom of the pot before the liquid gets hot enough to make the necessary steam for the pressure.

Unfortunately, because of the amount of liquid required for this dish, you can't use the pot's rack. A vegetable steamer has bigger feet and can sit at least 1 inch off the bottom of the pot.

1. Stir the broth, rice, onion, bell pepper strips, Cajun seasoning blend, and salt (if using) in a **6- or 8-quart Instant Pot.** Drop the butter pieces evenly over this mixture. Set a large, open vegetable steamer inside the pot. Put the sausage in the steamer. Lock the lid onto the pot.

2.

Set the machine for	Set the level for	The valve must be	And set the time for	If necessary, press
PRESSURE COOK	MAX	—	10 minutes with the KEEP WARM setting off	START
MEAT/STEW, PRESSURE COOK, or MANUAL	HIGH	Closed	12 minutes with the KEEP WARM setting off	START

3. Use the **quick-release method** to bring the pot's pressure back to normal but *do not open the cooker.* Set aside for 10 minutes, then unlatch the lid and open the pot. Transfer the sausages to a nearby cutting board and slice into 1-inch pieces. Stir into the rice mixture before serving.

Beyond

- Rather than using a purchased Cajun blend, substitute ½ teaspoon mild paprika, ½ teaspoon garlic powder, ½ teaspoon onion powder, ½ teaspoon dried thyme, ½ teaspoon cayenne, and ½ teaspoon table salt.

- If you can find only a large kielbasa ring, rather than links, you can steam it in the steamer for the same amount of time as the links.

 Using a **–20°F CHEST FREEZER?** There is no difference in cooking times.

Braised Ham and Carrots

6–8 servings

One 12-ounce can ginger ale

One <u>frozen</u> 3- to 3½-pound boneless smoked ham (not a country-style ham; and gluten-free, if that is a concern)

1 tablespoon ginger or orange marmalade

1–2 pounds "baby" carrots

Stock up on hams when you see them on sale after Easter or New Year's Day. If you've got one (or more!) in the freezer, you've got a ham dinner in the making in much less time than it would take in the oven. Braising a ham gives it a soft, meaty texture without any dried-out bits.

There's no better use of leftovers than making scrambled eggs with ham and onions. Or add diced ham to a soup or stew at the last minute for a hit of porky goodness.

Why is the ham cooked to a lower temperature than other pork dishes? Because a smoked ham is fully cooked and so has to reach only a slightly lower temperature for food safety.

1. Pour the ginger ale into a **6- or 8-quart Instant Pot.** Set the pot's rack (with the handles up) or a large, open vegetable steamer inside the pot. Set the frozen ham on the rack or in the steamer. Smear the marmalade on the meat. Lock the lid onto the pot.

2.

Set the machine for	Set the level for	The valve must be	And set the time for	If necessary, press
PRESSURE COOK	MAX	—	35 minutes with the KEEP WARM setting off	START
MEAT/STEW, PRESSURE COOK, or MANUAL	HIGH	Closed	45 minutes with the KEEP WARM setting off	START

3. When the machine has finished cooking, turn it off and let its pressure **return to normal naturally,** about 40 minutes. Unlatch the lid and open the cooker. Remove the rack or steamer from the (very hot!) cooker, letting the ham fall into the liquid below. Sprinkle the carrots all around the meat. Lock the lid back onto the pot.

4.

Set the machine for	Set the level for	The valve must be	And set the time for	If necessary, press
PRESSURE COOK	MAX	—	3 minutes with the KEEP WARM setting off	START
MEAT/STEW, PRESSURE COOK, or MANUAL	HIGH	Closed	5 minutes with the KEEP WARM setting off	START

5. Use the **quick-release method** to bring the pot's pressure back to normal. Again, unlatch the lid and open the cooker. Insert an instant-read meat thermometer into the thickest part of the ham without touching bone and make sure it registers at least 140°F. If not, scoop out the carrots with a slotted spoon, then lock the lid back on the pot and cook the ham at HIGH pressure for 5 minutes, followed by a **quick release.** Unlatch the lid and open the pot again.

6. Use tongs and a big metal spatula to transfer the ham to a nearby cutting board. Cool for a few minutes, then carve into thin slices or small chunks to serve with the carrots and perhaps some of the "juices" from the pot.

Beyond

- Unfortunately, the "juices" from a smoked ham are so salty that they are fine as briny pan juices on their own, but don't boil down well into a proper sauce. However, you can freeze those juices in small, sealed, ½-cup containers to add a little hammy, salty goodness to any pot of soup you make.

- The best garnish is mustard of any sort (honey mustard, deli mustard, whatever you like). And perhaps drizzle a little melted butter over the carrots.

 Using a **-20°F CHEST FREEZER?** Cook under pressure in step 2 for 45 minutes on the MAX setting or for 55 minutes on the HIGH setting. (The second cooking time under pressure remains unchanged.)

6

Fish and Shellfish

By our last count, we've published over 1,000 recipes for pressure cookers. The ones for fish and shellfish still catch us by surprise. It seems so strange to put something that cooks so quickly in a pressure cooker.

Yes, in other books we've often used the pot's pressure to build a deeply flavored sauce, then we've just cooked fish or shellfish in that sauce. But frankly, it makes a lot of sense to put frozen seafood right in the pot and let the machine work its magic. The seafood thaws as the pot comes to pressure, then cooks in no time.

A few words about "0 minutes": Some of these recipes ask you to set the pot for 0 minutes under pressure. In other words, the pot hits its high-pressure point, then instantly quits and starts to fall back off.

Here's the *big* problem: Not every model of Instant Pot can be set to 0 minutes. Most can; but a few can't. If yours cannot be set to 0 minutes, here's what you need to do: Set it for 1 minute at HIGH pressure, then don't leave the kitchen. You don't have to watch the pot obsessively, but do stick around. The minute the machine beeps, or flips from the word "on" to the number "1," or starts counting down from high pressure in some way, use the quick-release method to get rid of the pressure *or* turn the cooker off and let it come back to pressure naturally, whichever method the recipe requires. In other words, you're manually forcing the machine into a 0-minute cooking time so that the seafood won't be overcooked and mushy. And a better meal, even from frozen fare, is what this cookbook is all about.

Buttery Scallops

3–6 servings

½ cup chicken broth

¼ teaspoon baking soda

4 tablespoons (½ stick) butter

1 or 2 sprigs fresh oregano, parsley, rosemary, tarragon, or thyme

1–2 pounds <u>frozen</u> sea scallops

Poaching scallops right in butter is something you can do only in a pressure cooker. The butter would burn on the stovetop (or, at least, its milk solids would fall out of suspension and burn). By adding a little baking soda to the pot, you change the pH of the mixture and keep the butter solids from burning. We learned this technique from culinary genius Nathan Myhrvold and used it extensively in *The Instant Pot Bible* for creamy soups. Here, we've adapted it for frozen scallops.

This dish makes a wide range of number of servings because it really doesn't matter if you use 1 or 2 pounds of frozen sea scallops. The timing and technique are the same.

Consider serving these as an easy dinner over cooked white rice. Or halve (or quarter) each cooked scallop and serve them in their sauce with toothpicks for a much fancier cocktail hour.

1.

Press the button for	Set it for	Set the time for	If necessary, press
SAUTÉ	MEDIUM, NORMAL, or CUSTOM 300°F	10 minutes	START

2. Stir the broth and baking soda in a **6-quart Instant Pot.** Add the butter and herb sprig(s). Continue cooking, stirring often, until wisps of steam rise off the liquid. Turn off the SAUTÉ function. Put the frozen scallops in the pot. Lock the lid onto the cooker.

3.

Set the machine for	Set the level for	The valve must be	And set the time for	If necessary, press
PRESSURE COOK	MAX	—	0 minutes (see page 163) with the KEEP WARM setting off	START
PRESSURE COOK or MANUAL	HIGH	Closed	0 minutes (see page 163) with the KEEP WARM setting off	START

4. When the machine has finished cooking, turn it off and let its pressure **return to normal naturally** for 1 minute. Then use the **quick-release method** to get rid of the pot's residual pressure. Unlatch the lid and open the cooker. Use a slotted spoon to transfer the scallops to a serving platter; spoon lots of the sauce from the pot over them.

 Using a **-20°F CHEST FREEZER?** There is no difference in cooking times.

Beyond

- For an **8-quart Instant Pot,** you *must* double all the ingredients *except* the scallops. You *can* use anywhere from 1 to 3 pounds of frozen sea scallops in the larger machine.

- Garnish the scallops and their sauce with lots of ground black pepper.

- For more flavor, add up to ½ teaspoon Old Bay seasoning to the pot with the baking soda.

- For a richer sauce, use a slotted spoon to transfer the scallops to a serving platter in step 4 and tent them with foil. Turn the pot's SAUTÉ function to HIGH, MORE, or CUSTOM 400°F. Add ¼ cup heavy cream and boil the sauce until it's reduced to about half its original volume, 3–4 minutes. Turn off the SAUTÉ function and pour the sauce over the scallops to serve.

- Substitute frozen peeled and deveined large raw shrimp (15–20 per pound) for the scallops.

Sweet and Sour Shrimp

4–6 servings

1 cup canned, drained pineapple chunks in juice, plus ¼ cup juice from the can

½ cup chicken, vegetable, or fish broth

¼ cup regular or reduced-sodium soy sauce or tamari

¼ cup granulated white sugar

¼ cup unseasoned rice vinegar, (see headnote on page 92); or 3 tablespoons apple cider vinegar

1 tablespoon peeled and minced fresh ginger

2 teaspoons peeled and minced garlic

¼ teaspoon red pepper flakes

1½ pounds <u>frozen</u> peeled and deveined raw medium shrimp (30–35 per pound)

1 pound (4 to 5 cups) <u>frozen</u> unseasoned stir-fry vegetable blend (any seasoning packet discarded)

2 tablespoons cornstarch

It takes several ingredients to create a good sweet-and-sour sauce. But the payoff is worth it when the meal is so tasty! Remember that shrimp are sold by the number it takes to make a pound, and words like "large" or "jumbo" are mere window dressing. To get the timing right, make sure you have shrimp that are sized at 35 count (or maybe 30) per pound.

Also, just to make sure things are clear, buy frozen *raw* shrimp, not cooked "cocktail" shrimp.

1. Stir the drained pineapple chunks (but not the juice), the broth, soy sauce or tamari, sugar, vinegar, ginger, garlic, and red pepper flakes in a **6-quart Instant Pot.** Add the frozen shrimp and vegetables to the pot and stir well. Lock the lid onto the pot.

2.

Set the machine for	Set the level for	The valve must be	And set the time for	If necessary, press
PRESSURE COOK	MAX	—	0 minutes (see page 163) with the KEEP WARM setting off	START
PRESSURE COOK or MANUAL	HIGH	Closed	0 minutes (see page 163) with the KEEP WARM setting off	START

3. Use the **quick-release method** to bring the pot's pressure back to normal. Unlatch the lid and open the cooker.

4.

Press the button for	Set it for	Set the time for	If necessary, press
SAUTÉ	MEDIUM, NORMAL, or CUSTOM 300°F	5 minutes	START

5. As the sauce comes to a simmer, whisk the reserved ¼ cup pineapple juice and the cornstarch in a small bowl until smooth. Stir this mixture into the simmering sauce. Cook, stirring almost constantly, until thickened, less than 1 minute. Turn off the SAUTÉ function and remove the (hot!) insert from the pot to prevent the shrimp from overcooking. Pour the shrimp and all their sauce into a serving bowl.

 Using a **–20°F CHEST FREEZER?** There is no difference in cooking times.

Beyond

- For an **8-quart Instant Pot,** you must increase all the ingredients by 50 percent.

- For more flavor, add ¼ teaspoon five-spice powder to the pot with the red pepper flakes.

- The shrimp and their sauce can be ladled over cooked white or brown rice, particularly a long-grain rice. Or serve them over a bed of wilted spinach or kale.

- For a lot more flavor (and a lot more mess), substitute frozen deveined but peel-on shrimp. The shells do make up added weight, so we suggest you cut the number of servings strictly to four. And you'll have to peel and eat the shrimp with your fingers. But the additional briny punch might be worth it.

- Substitute 1½ pounds frozen sea scallops for the shrimp.

Shrimp Creole

4 servings

One 14-ounce can diced
tomatoes packed in juice with
chiles (1¾ cups)

1 cup chicken, vegetable, or fish
broth

1 cup <u>frozen</u> chopped onion; or
1 medium yellow or white
onion, peeled and chopped

1 cup thinly sliced celery
(3 medium stalks)

4 ounces (1 cup) <u>frozen</u> bell
pepper strips; or 1 medium
green or red bell pepper,
stemmed, cored, and chopped

1½ tablespoons dried Creole
seasoning blend

1 tablespoon Worcestershire
sauce (gluten-free, if that's a
concern)

2 teaspoons peeled and minced
garlic

2 pounds <u>frozen</u> peeled and
deveined raw medium shrimp
(30 to 35 per pound)

Here's a regional dish from the Gulf Coast that's become an all-American favorite: shrimp with a spicy tomato-based sauce. The technique here is a bit different from the previous seafood recipes: You build the sauce under pressure, then add the shrimp for a second cooking. The point is to force the flavors to blend as the tomatoes almost melt into the sauce. If you added the shrimp from the get-go, they'd get overcooked before the tomatoes turned into sauce.

1. Mix the tomatoes, broth, onion, celery, bell pepper, Creole seasoning blend, Worcestershire sauce, and garlic in a **6- or 8-quart Instant Pot.** Lock the lid onto the pot.

2.

Set the machine for	Set the level for	The valve must be	And set the time for	If necessary, press
PRESSURE COOK	MAX	——	3 minutes with the KEEP WARM setting off	START
PRESSURE COOK or MANUAL	HIGH	Closed	5 minutes with the KEEP WARM setting off	START

3. Use the **quick-release method** to bring the pot's pressure back to normal. Unlatch the lid and open the cooker. Stir in the shrimp. Lock the lid back onto the pot.

4.

Set the machine for	Set the level for	The valve must be	And set the time for	If necessary, press
PRESSURE COOK	MAX	—	0 minutes (see page 163) with the KEEP WARM setting off	START
PRESSURE COOK or MANUAL	HIGH	Closed	0 minutes (see page 163) with the KEEP WARM setting off	START

5. Again, use the **quick-release method** to bring the pot's pressure back to normal. Unlatch the lid and open the cooker. Stir well before serving.

 Using a **-20°F CHEST FREEZER?** There is no difference in cooking times.

Beyond

- For a thicker sauce, use a slotted spoon to remove the shrimp from the pot in step 5. Turn the SAUTÉ function to MEDIUM, NORMAL, or CUSTOM 300°F. Bring the sauce to a simmer, then whisk in 2 tablespoons tomato paste. Cook, whisking all the while, to thicken, about 1 minute. Turn off the SAUTÉ function and ladle the sauce over the shrimp.

- If you don't want to use a purchased *Creole* seasoning blend, see our alternate blend in the *Beyond* for the Buttery Cajun Rice with Smoked Sausage recipe on page 159. Yes, this blend is Cajun, not Creole—but it will do nicely here.

- Serve this dish over cooked, long-grain white rice. Or try something different and serve it over cooked millet, which has an earthy, slightly bitter taste that matches well with the rich sauce.

Shrimp Scampi

4 servings

¾ cup dry white wine (such as Chardonnay) or dry vermouth

2 tablespoons butter

2 tablespoons olive oil

4 teaspoons peeled and minced garlic

½ teaspoon dried oregano

½ teaspoon red pepper flakes

2 pounds frozen peeled and deveined raw medium shrimp (30 to 35 per pound)

Look no further for the quickest shrimp supper — or the best fare to be served with toothpicks at your next cocktail party. "Scampi" traditionally refers to a specific type of shellfish, but in North America the term has come to mean a garlicky, buttery sauce for shellfish.

Because of the butter and oil in this dish, we recommend only using frozen *peeled and deveined* shrimp. Peeling them after they're cooked can get messy!

1. Mix the wine, butter, oil, garlic, oregano, and red pepper flakes in a **6-quart Instant Pot.** Stir in the shrimp and lock the lid onto the pot.

2.

Set the machine for	Set the level for	The valve must be	And set the time for	If necessary, press
PRESSURE COOK	MAX	—	0 minutes (see page 163) with the KEEP WARM setting off	START
PRESSURE COOK or MANUAL	HIGH	Closed	0 minutes (see page 163) with the KEEP WARM setting off	START

3. Use the **quick-release method** to bring the pot's pressure back to normal. Unlatch the lid and open the cooker. Pour the hot shrimp and sauce into a bowl to serve.

Beyond

- For an **8-quart Instant Pot,** you must increase all the ingredients *except* the shrimp by 50 percent. However, you *can* increase the shrimp by 50 percent as well, if you like.

- You can make this dish with giant shrimp, such as frozen U-10s (that is, under 10 shrimp per pound) or even U-5s. Note that you'll need to set the pressure to 1 minute for either MAX or HIGH, followed by a **quick release.**

- Shrimp scampi is served over pasta in lots of Italian-American restaurants. We recommend cooked and drained angel hair pasta.

❄️ Using a **-20°F CHEST FREEZER?** There is no difference in cooking times.

Simple Steamed Salmon Fillets

2 servings

Over the last year, we've seen a lot of worry on social media about how to cook frozen salmon fillets in an Instant Pot. And no wonder! The fillets can be overcooked in a flash. We find the best technique is to steam them on a rack because they don't sit in the liquid (which can break them apart, especially during the furious boil inside the pot when the pressure is released).

Our timing here is for medium-rare to medium salmon fillets. If you like them cooked more thoroughly, add 1 minute to the timing for either the MAX or the HIGH setting. But note: The size of these salmon fillets (6 ounces each) is very important for the timing given; see the *Beyond* if you have larger fillets.

1. Pour the water or wine into a **6-quart Instant Pot.** Set the pot's rack (with the handles up) or a large, open vegetable steamer inside the pot. Set the fillets skin-side down on the rack or in the steamer, arranging them so they overlap as little as possible (do not stack them). Set two barely overlapping lemon slices on each fillet. Sprinkle the fish and lemon slices evenly with the pepper and salt. Lock the lid onto the cooker.

2.

Set the machine for	Set the level for	The valve must be	And set the time for	If necessary, press
PRESSURE COOK	MAX	—	5 minutes with the KEEP WARM setting off	START
MEAT/ STEW, PRESSURE COOK, or MANUAL	HIGH	Closed	6 minutes with the KEEP WARM setting off	START

3. Use the **quick-release method** to bring the pot's pressure back to normal. Unlatch the lid and open the cooker. Use a metal spatula to transfer the fillets one by one to serving plates.

1 cup water or dry white wine of any sort

Two frozen 6-ounce skin-on salmon fillets

4 paper-thin fresh lemon slices, any seeds removed

½ teaspoon ground black pepper

¼ teaspoon table salt

Beyond

- For an **8-quart Instant Pot,** you must use 1½ cups water or white wine. You can also use three frozen 6-ounce fillets. (Four would be too many and begin to stack on top of each other.)

- You can add lots more flavor by sprinkling ½ teaspoon dried seasoning blend on each fillet before adding the lemon slices.

- If you've got frozen 8-ounce fillets, cook them at MAX for 6 minutes or at HIGH for 7 minutes, followed by a **quick release.**

- These salmon fillets are great over riced cauliflower or on top of a kale Caesar salad.

❄ Using a **-20°F CHEST FREEZER?** There is no difference in cooking times.

Salmon with Creamy Mustard Sauce

4 servings

½ cup dry white wine, such as Chardonnay

½ cup chicken, vegetable, or fish broth

½ cup frozen chopped onion; or 1 small yellow or white onion, peeled and chopped

2 tablespoons chopped fresh dill fronds, or 1½ teaspoons dried dill

1 tablespoon Dijon mustard

Four frozen 6-ounce skin-on salmon fillets

2 tablespoons heavy or light cream (but *not* "fat-free" cream)

2 teaspoons cornstarch

Light but creamy, satisfying but not overly indulgent, this salmon supper is a great dish to serve to guests on the weekend when you want something a little fancier than a stew or a braise. The fillets will be medium-rare to medium. If you'd like the fish more done, add 1 minute to either the MAX or the HIGH cooking time.

One note: Because there are four fillets here and they overlap each other on the rack, the timing is a little longer than the previous salmon fillet recipe.

1. Stir the wine, broth, onion, dill, and mustard in a **6-quart Instant Pot.** Set the pot's rack (with the handles up) or a large, open vegetable steamer inside the pot. Overlap the salmon fillets on the rack or in the pot, sort of like shingles, with the thin part of one under the thicker part of another. Lock the lid onto the pot.

2.

Set the machine for	Set the level for	The valve must be	And set the time for	If necessary, press
PRESSURE COOK	MAX	—	6 minutes with the KEEP WARM setting off	START
PRESSURE COOK or MANUAL	HIGH	Closed	8 minutes with the KEEP WARM setting off	START

3. Use the **quick-release method** to bring the pot's pressure back to normal. Unlatch the lid and open the cooker. Use a metal spatula to transfer the fillets to serving plates or a platter. (If you've used the pot's rack, you might be able to grasp the handles with silicone cooking mitts, then lift the whole thing out with the fillets on it. It's a balancing act — and difficult to pull off when the pot's hot.)

4.

Press the button for	Set it for	Set the time for	If necessary, press
SAUTÉ	MEDIUM, NORMAL, or CUSTOM 300°F	5 minutes	START

5. As the sauce comes to a simmer, whisk the cream and cornstarch in a small bowl or teacup until smooth. Stir this slurry into the pot and cook, stirring constantly, until the sauce thickens a bit, less than 1 minute. Turn off the SAUTÉ function and ladle the sauce over the salmon fillets to serve.

 Using a **−20°F CHEST FREEZER?** There is no difference in cooking times.

Beyond

- For an **8-quart Instant Pot,** you must increase all the ingredients *except* the salmon fillets by 50 percent. However, you *can* increase the frozen salmon fillets to up to six of them shingled on the rack.

- Serve the fillets and sauce over buttery noodles.

- Decent fish broth remains the grail for many cooks. Clam juice can work, but it's very salty and the flavor is most often nothing but dull brininess. There are fish-stock bases sold in high-end supermarkets, often in the freezer case. These must be diluted to render a thinner broth. Or you can make fish stock in the Instant Pot; we have a recipe in *The Instant Pot Bible.* You can't believe how terrific this salmon recipe (and others) will taste if you've squirreled away fish stock in small containers in your freezer.

Cod Fillets with Tomatoes and Zucchini

4 servings

One 28-ounce can diced tomatoes packed in juice (3½ cups)

10 ounces (2 cups) <u>frozen</u> sliced zucchini; or 1 medium zucchini, sliced into ¼-inch-thick rounds

½ cup <u>frozen</u> chopped onion; or 1 small yellow or white onion, peeled and chopped

One 4-ounce jar diced pimientos (do not drain)

1 tablespoon dried Provençal or Mediterranean seasoning blend

Four <u>frozen</u> 6-ounce skinless cod fillets

The flavors here are sort of like ratatouille, but minus the eggplant. However, the final consistency of the vegetables surrounding the fish is more like a sauce because the vegetables are just about melted down by the pot's pressure in the two-step cooking process. If you find the sauce is too thin after cooking, remove the fish from the pot and boil the sauce down with the SAUTÉ function on MEDIUM, NORMAL, or CUSTOM 300°F for a few minutes. Even so, we find that a little bit of, well, wateriness in the sauce brings a lightness to the overall dish.

One note: It may seem strange, particularly in an 8-quart cooker, that there's no additional liquid with the tomatoes and other vegetables. The zucchini will throw off so much liquid that the pot will come to pressure without any burn notice. Just remember to use only diced tomatoes *packed in juice*.

1. Stir the tomatoes, zucchini, onion, pimientos, and seasoning blend in a **6- or 8-quart Instant Pot.** Lock the lid onto the cooker.

2.

Set the machine for	Set the level for	The valve must be	And set the time for	If necessary, press
PRESSURE COOK	MAX	—	3 minutes with the KEEP WARM setting off	START
PRESSURE COOK or MANUAL	HIGH	Closed	4 minutes with the KEEP WARM setting off	START

3. Use the **quick-release method** to bring the pot's pressure back to normal. Unlatch the lid and open the cooker. Nestle the cod fillets into the sauce. Lock the lid back onto the pot.

4.

Set the machine for	Set the level for	The valve must be	And set the time for	If necessary, press
PRESSURE COOK	MAX	—	5 minutes with the KEEP WARM setting off	START
PRESSURE COOK or MANUAL	HIGH	Closed	6 minutes with the KEEP WARM setting off	START

5. Again, use the **quick-release method** to bring the pot's pressure back to normal. Unlatch the lid and open the cooker. Use a large cooking spoon to transfer the fish and sauce to serving bowls.

 Using a **-20°F CHEST FREEZER?** There is no difference in cooking times.

Beyond

- If you don't want to use a Provençal or Mediterranean seasoning blend, substitute 1 teaspoon lemon pepper seasoning, 1 teaspoon dried marjoram, and 1 teaspoon dried thyme.

- Garnish each serving with 1 tablespoon butter or a generous drizzle of extra-virgin olive oil.

- Substitute four frozen 6-ounce halibut or tilapia fillets for the cod.

- Garnish with finely grated lemon zest and/or drained and rinsed capers. Or skip those and garnish each serving with a little tapenade. And don't forget garlic toast!

Butter-Poached Mahi-Mahi

4 servings

½ teaspoon mild paprika

½ teaspoon onion powder

½ teaspoon table salt

½ teaspoon ground black pepper

1½ cups water

Four frozen 6-ounce, 5- or 6-inch-long skinless mahi-mahi fillets

8 tablespoons (1 stick) butter

This recipe is the only "PiP" (that is, in Instant Pot terminology, "pot in pot") recipe in this book. We found that technique too fussy for a book about getting dinner on the table straight from the freezer. However, in this one case, our last recipe, we felt the extra step was warranted because mahi-mahi is a thicker, meatier fish and takes longer to cook. It's also expensive and we wanted to make sure the fish remains moist and delicate. When the fillets were set right on the cooker's bottom or even in a rack, they tended to turn mushy, given the time the pot needs to stay under pressure to thaw and cook the fish.

Watch the size of the frozen fillets. They must lie flat in a 7-inch baking dish.

1. Mix the paprika, onion powder, salt, and pepper in a small bowl until uniform.

2. Pour the water into a **6- or 8-quart Instant Pot.** Set the pot's rack (with the handles up) or a pressure-safe trivet inside the pot. Set a pressure-safe 7-inch round baking dish in the cooker. (A springform pan will leak and should not be used.) Stack the fillets in the dish, sprinkling each with an even coating of the spice mixture (about ½ teaspoon on each). Set the stick of butter on top of the fillets and lock the lid onto the pot.

3.

Set the machine for	Set the level for	The valve must be	And set the time for	If necessary, press
PRESSURE COOK	MAX	—	7 minutes with the KEEP WARM setting off	START
PRESSURE COOK or MANUAL	HIGH	Closed	8 minutes with the KEEP WARM setting off	START

4. Use the **quick-release method** to bring the pot's pressure back to normal. Unlatch the lid and open the cooker. Use silicone cooking mitts or thick hot pads to transfer the baking dish to a heat-safe work surface. Use a metal spatula to transfer the fillets one by one to serving plates or a platter. Spoon some (or all) of the buttery "sauce" in the baking dish over the fish.

 Using a **–20°F CHEST FREEZER?** There is no difference in cooking times.

Beyond

- If desired, substitute four frozen 6-ounce, 5- or 6-inch-long halibut or tilapia fillets for the mahi-mahi.

- This dish is great over a bed of steamed asparagus (particularly with all that butter sauce).

Acknowledgments

When you're an author, you thank and you thank and you thank and it still doesn't add up to all everyone does to make it look as if you produced a book on your own.

First off, thanks to everyone in all the **Facebook groups** who support our work, make our recipes, post them, write us, inspire us, and cheer us on to make the best book we can.

Thanks, too, to **Eric Medsker,** the best photographer we know, the one who's done our last seven books (although this thing about *stirred* martinis is really troubling). And to **Victoria Maiolo**, the prop stylist who worked so tirelessly to have a zillion plates and bowls on set so we could take multiples of some shots.

At Little, Brown, we owe our ongoing gratitude to **Reagan Arthur,** our publisher; **Craig Young,** our deputy publisher; **Jules Horbachevsky** and **Elora Weil** for the book's PR initiatives; **Kim Sheu** for marketing strategies; **Laura Palese** for the book's design; **Julianna Lee** and **Kapo Ng** for the cover art; **Lisa Ferris**, the book's production manager; **Jayne Yaffe Kemp,** its production editor; **Amy Novick**, its indexer; **Allan Fallow** and **Pat Jalbert-Levine,** its proofreaders; **Michael Gaudet** for digital production; and **Laura Mamelok** for working on its foreign rights.

And we owe more than gratitude, much more, to **Mike Szczerban**, about the best editor any writers could want (except the part about leftover lentils and squirt cheese); and to **Nicky Guerreiro**, his associate editor, who can apparently read almost anything and cogently reply to it in, oh, ten seconds flat. And there are not enough ways to thank **Deri Reed**, the copyeditor of our dreams, whom we'd write into our contracts if we could.

We owe more than our gratitude, more like our careers, to our agent, **Susan Ginsburg**, at Writers House. (For twenty-two years? But aren't we all, like, thirty-five?) And to her former assistant, **Stacy Testa,** now gone on to greener pastures; and her current assistant, **Catherine Bradshaw,** who has no idea what she's in for.

Index